**On the cover:** Rose window, Maryknoll chapel, Maryknoll, N.Y., depicting the descent of the Holy Spirit in the Cenacle, viewed as though entered through the Cross.

# The Spirit and the Bride Say, "Come!"

## Mary's Role in the New Pentecost

GERALD J. FARRELL, M.M.
and
GEORGE W. KOSICKI, C.S.B.

AMI Press
Mountain View Road
Asbury, N.J. 08802

**NIHIL OBSTAT:**

Rev. Msgr. William Maguire, S.T.D.

Having been advised by competent authority that this book contains no teaching contrary to the Faith and Morals as taught by the Church, I approve its publication according to the Decree of the Sacred Congregation for the Doctrine of the Faith. This approval does not necessarily indicate any promotion or advocacy of the theological or devotional content of the work.

**IMPRIMATUR:**

† John C. Reiss, J.C.D.
Bishop of Trenton

© Copyright, AMI Press, 1981

First Printing:  10,000 December 1981
Second Printing:  10,000 August 1982 (with Appendix)

**ISBN 0-911988-41-6**

# Dedication

We give heartfelt thanks to God for the Marians of the Immaculate Conception, at Stockbridge, Massachusetts, who so graciously hosted us for a time of extended retreat. It was in this prayerful and beautiful environment that we wrote this book on the role of Mary in the new Pentecost.

# Table of Contents

viii

# Prologue

# Prayer of
# Pope John XXIII [1]

"Divine Spirit, renew your wonders in this our age as in a new Pentecost, and grant that your Church, praying perseveringly and insistently with one heart and mind together with Mary, the Mother of Jesus, and guided by blessed Peter, may increase the reign of the Divine Savior, the reign of truth and justice, the reign of love and peace. Amen."

*This prayer of Pope John XXIII used in convoking the Second Vatican Council gives a prophetic vision of the new Pentecost in the Church, expressing it in capsule form. It serves as a battle cry in this time of spiritual warfare for the coming of the Kingdom.*

## NOTES

1. **Humanae Salutis,** December 25, 1961. This text is translated from the original Latin by the authors. All other quotations from the Second Vatican Council are from **The Documents of Vatican II,** W. M. Abbott, General Editor, Herder & Herder, New York, N.Y. 10016, 1966.

# General Introduction

The last chapter of the final book of the Bible ends with a united plea for the coming of the Lord Jesus. Together "The Spirit and the Bride say, 'Come!' " (Rev. 22:17). The coming of the Lord Jesus is in answer to the plea of *both* the Spirit and the Bride, i.e., the Church.

The *Spirit* has been pleading and has been acting in a sovereign way in this our age through the Pentecostal renewal of the Churches. At the beginning of this century, people from various evangelical and holiness denominations were baptized in the Holy Spirit with the accompanying gifts. The Pentecostal Churches that came out of this experience increased more rapidly in proportion than any other Christian Churches in this century. In 1957 the Pentecostal renewal began in the Anglican churches as pastors and congregations were baptized in the Holy Spirit. In 1967 the Holy Spirit touched a small group of Catholic students from Duquesne University on a weekend retreat. As a result of this sovereign act of God various other groups of Catholics were baptized in the Holy Spirit and came together for prayer and sharing. From the early groups at South Bend, Indiana, and Ann Arbor, Michigan, the "charismatic renewal" within the Catholic Church quickly spread to millions of Catholics around the world.

Only two years after this renewal began in the
Catholic Church, the National Conference of Catholic
Bishops of the U.S.A. publically encouraged it. In 1975
the Holy Father too gave it public encouragement as
10,000 leaders and people gathered in Rome for the
International Conference on the Charismatic Renewal
in the Catholic Church. In 1976 Archbishop Bernardin
personally and officially as President of the National
Conference of Catholic Bishops of the U.S.A. gave it his
endorsement.

But despite its amazing growth and despite these
official endorsements, the Catholic charismatic renewal
appears to have reached a peak and begun to decline.
We believe that this peaking phenomenon is not a sign
of the charismatic renewal's failure, but rather that it is
part of God's plan for the full renewal of his Church.
We believe that this wave of charismatic renewal is
beginning to ebb only in order that a new wave of
renewal may follow, one that will involve a new
sovereign act of God, that will embrace all of
Christianity, and that will lead to the new Pentecost
prayed for by Pope John XXIII.

As will be described in Chapter I, the Catholic
Church as Bride of Christ was invited by the Spirit
during the pontificate of Pope Leo XIII to full renewal in
the Spirit. Unfortunately, it failed to respond
adequately to that invitation. Again, through John
XXIII it was invited to full renewal, an invitation which
was initially taken up by the Second Vatican Council
and which began to bear fruit in its teachings. From its
beginning the purpose of the Catholic charismatic
renewal has been the implementation of Vatican II
through the guidance and power of the Holy Spirit. We
believe that the charismatic renewal has served the
Catholic Church powerfully and will continue to serve
it as a prophetic movement pointing to the new

Pentecost. And yet it has involved only a very small part of the Church. How, then, is the Church, the Bride, to be fully prepared in order that it can say wholeheartedly with the Spirit, "Come!"?

We believe that a prophecy given at the charismatic conference in St. Peter's Basilica during the Holy Year of 1975 pointed to the answer. It spoke of a new age dawning for the Church. And it spoke of entering into a different type of combat for which a new wisdom, a new power, and a new understanding of God's ways would be needed. We believe that the answer itself was provided three years later by the newly elected Pope John Paul II when, from the central balcony of the same basilica in the first moments of his pontificate he entrusted himself and the whole Church to "the Mother of Christ and of the Church" in order "...to start anew on this road of history and of the Church..." His papal motto, "Totus Tuus," ("[I am] All Yours"), signifies his personal consecration to Mary. On each of his pilgrimages as well as in Rome, he has consecrated the entire Church to Mary. And in his letter of Holy Thursday, 1979, addressed to all the priests of the Church, he consecrated each of them to Mary, strongly urging them to ratify this consecration personally.

We believe that by these actions our Holy Father is entrusting to Mary, the Mother of the Church, the clothing of the Bride with a new wisdom, a new power, and a new understanding of God's ways. The evidence to support this belief comes from many sources: Sacred Scripture, Church Councils, Papal teachings, private revelations approved by the Church, and in the writings of saints and scholars. We believe that consecration to Mary is an essential step toward the sovereign act needed to bring about the new Pentecost. This step of consecration is a needed preparation for Calvary where in a corporate way we will experience the crucifixion as did Jesus, our Head. The Cross is the source of the power both of resurrection and of Pentecost. From Calvary we will move to the Cenacle where, as the Bride in union with the Spirit, "together with Mary, the Mother of Jesus, and guided by blessed Peter" (cf Prologue) we will pray, "Come, Lord Jesus!"

The acceptance of the role of Mary, the Mother of Jesus, in the renewal of the Church by the various denominations and even by some Catholics will in itself require a sovereign act of God. Mary is the personal gift of the Lord Jesus to his Church along with the gifts of the Eucharist and Peter. These three gifts have been treasured and preserved by the Catholic Church in order to be shared with all Christians. But historical events and cultural prejudices have made it difficult for some to appreciate these treasures and to accept them. Their acceptance, then, will be part of the sovereign act of God.

This book focuses on the gift of Mary.

The reflections contained in it have grown out of several current events:

* The ever-worsening travail in the Church and the world,
* The changes taking place in the charismatic renewal as it grows, matures and now peaks,
* The clear witness and example given by Pope John Paul II in entrusting the Church to Mary as he leads it to renewal.

In these reflections on Mary and the new Pentecost we describe Mary's role in the renewal of the Church as one of *model and mother*. These two terms are pivotal concepts in the all-important Chapter VIII of the Second Vatican Council's document on the Church, *Lumen Gentium*, and are used here to describe Mary's role in the preparation of the Church for the new Pentecost. As *model*, Mary already is what the Church is yet to be, as *mother,* Mary is the active agent in union with the Spirit in accomplishing the new Pentecost.

The background for these reflections is presented in two earlier books by G. W. Kosicki, *Intercessory Prayer: Rediscovery of the Priestly Dimension* and *Pilgrimage and Purification: the Church in Travail in the 80's.*[1]

## NOTES

1. Crux, 75 Champlain St., Albany, NY 12204, 1978 and 1980.

As Jesus was crucified so share the Church be crucified. So that as Christ Rose from the Dead, So will His church - The 'new' church needs a new Pentecost - as did the 'new' church for the beginning - (Fr.)

**Part One**

# The Spirit Says,
# "Come!"

In Part I, we look at the sovereign acts of the Holy Spirit occurring in the Pentecostal Movement of this century. Beginning with what the Holy Spirit has done among the poor in spirit at the turn of the century, we trace this movement until its eventual entrance into the Catholic Church, examine the present phenomenon of peaking in the renewal and then look forward to the future in the light of prophecy. The focus of Part I, then, is on the Spirit and his work of renewing the Church.

# Chapter I

# Sovereign Acts
# of the Holy Spirit
# in the 20th Century
# Pentecostal Movement

Between 1895 and 1903, Blessed Sister Elena Guerra, foundress of the Oblate Sisters of the Holy Spirit in Italy, wrote twelve confidential letters to Pope Leo XIII asking that he foster devotion to the Holy Spirit so that the Church might be transformed into a praying and universal Cenacle. She was inspired by the Holy Spirit in this prophetic mission and helped by her spiritual director Bishop Giovanni Volpi. Pope Leo, recognizing the authenticity of her mission, responded by the publication of *Provida Matris Caritate* asking for a solemn novena to the Holy Spirit prior to Pentecost to be celebrated by the whole Church. In 1897, he published his encyclical on the Holy Spirit, *Divinum illud munus,* again prescribing the celebration of the novena for Pentecost in all parish churches of the world. Unfortunately, the response to the novena was poor. Pope Leo then sent a private letter to the bishops of the world, along with a copy of the encyclical, deploring the fact that many of the clergy thought the novena was to be held only for the year 1897. It ended by saying: "His Holiness nourishes the sure hope that the bishops and clergy will respond, with God's help in such a matter, with industry and alacrity."

In a letter dated October 15, 1900, Sister Elena suggested that Pope Leo begin the first new year of the

4

new century by singing "Come, Holy Spirit," in the name of the whole Church, which he did.[1]

It is an interesting fact that just one year later, on the night of December 31, 1900, to be exact, in Topeka, Kansas, Rev. Charles Parham prayed with Agnes Ozman to be baptized in the Holy Spirit, an occasion generally accepted as the beginning of the Pentecostal movement. The request and prayer of Pope Leo XIII received only a half-hearted response by the shepherds of the Catholic Church, and so the Lord once again turned to the "little ones" and poured out his Spirit. The students at the Bible School in Topeka, Kansas, were ready; they were a humble, praying people, earnestly seeking the Holy Spirit and for a sign of his presence. While studying the Acts of the Apostles and praying for the Holy Spirit, they experienced his presence and power along with the sign of the gifts of tongues and prophecy.

The Pentecostal churches that developed out of this sovereign act of the Spirit grew dramatically and became the third largest group of Christians after Catholics and Protestants. The Pentecostal movement continued among the simple and little people. Those who experienced the baptism in the Holy Spirit were regularly not accepted in their own churches and were forced to join other churches or form their own. It wasn't until 1957 that the renewal began to touch the mainline Protestant churches, but this time those baptized in the Holy Spirit were allowed to remain members of their churches.

The call of Pope Leo XIII to beseech the Holy Spirit was picked up explicitly by Pope John XXIII in April, 1959, on the occasion of the beatification of Sister Elena Guerra, whom he called "the Apostle of the Holy Spirit." In addressing the pilgrims of her home town he said, "Her message is always relevant. We are all aware, in fact, of the need for a continued effusion of the Holy Spirit, as of a new Pentecost." On the occasion of convoking the Second Vatican Council, Pope John once again took up this theme, praying, "Divine Spirit, renew your wonders in this our age, as in a new Pentecost...."[2]

In February, 1967, within a few years after the completion of the Second Vatican Council, a group of students from Duquesne University in Pittsburgh gathered for a weekend retreat on the Holy Spirit. It had been organized by their professor of liturgy and by a graduate student of the university. On Saturday evening of the retreat, one of the students left the birthday party they were having and went to the chapel. While praying before the Blessed Sacrament, she was overwhelmed by the presence of the Lord. Others soon joined her and all experienced the same power of the Holy Spirit. From this "Duquesne weekend," the mainstream of this Pentecostal renewal in the Catholic Church spread quickly to friends at the University of Notre Dame, then to East Lansing, and later to Ann Arbor. From these centers this renewal, which came to be known as the Catholic charismatic renewal, spread within a few years around the whole world.[3]

### The Discernment of the Charismatic Renewal by our Chief Shepherds

*Pope Paul VI*, during the Holy Year of 1975, addressed ten thousand participants of the International Conference on the Catholic Charismatic Renewal assembled in St. Peter's Basilica, Rome (May 19, 1975) as follows:

"This authentic desire to situate yourselves in the Church is the authentic sign of the action of the Holy Spirit.... How could this 'spiritual renewal' not be a 'chance' for the Church and the world? And how, in this case could one not

6

take all the means to ensure that it remains so?....Beloved sons and daughters, with the help of the Lord, strong in the intercession of Mary, the Mother of the Church, and in communion of faith, charity and of the apostolate with your pastors, you will be sure of not deceiving yourselves. And thus you will contribute for your part, to the renewal of the Church... You have gathered here in Rome under the sign of the Holy Year; you are striving in union with the whole Church for renewal—spiritual renewal, authentic renewal, Catholic renewal, renewal in the Holy Spirit. We are pleased to see signs of this renewal: a taste for prayer, contemplation, praising God, attentiveness to the grace of the Holy Spirit, and more assiduous reading of the Sacred Scriptures. We know likewise that you wish to open your hearts to reconciliation with God and your fellowmen.... This is a day of resolve: to open yourselves to the Holy Spirit, to remove what is opposed to his action, and to proclaim in the Christian authenticity of our lives that Jesus is Lord.''[4]

The *Bishops of the United States* have officially encouraged the charismatic renewal. Archbishop Bernardin addressed the National Conference on the Charismatic Renewal held at the University of Notre Dame on May 28, 1976, saying:

"I want to endorse the good that the charismatic movement is producing and encourage those of you in the movement to continue to open yourselves to the power of the Holy Spirit. I can give the same encouragement not only from a personal point of view, but also officially as President of the National Conference of Catholic Bishops.... So it is both officially and personally that I am pleased to encourage you to continued growth in the Spirit and continued dedication to the Lord Jesus. I wish to give you encouragement and support since I know that a life of total dedication to the Lord is not always easy. Jesus promised joy and peace, but he also promised the cross which brings suffering and rejection....

"I encourage you to be fully charismatic— that is, fully filled with the gifts of the Spirit— especially the gift of being able to exhort and minister to one another, the gift of prayer, the gift of discerning the Spirit working in many ways in the Church, and above all the gift of unselfish love....

"The hierarchy welcomes and needs your enthusiasm and renewed spirituality, and you need the bishops, those who have been appointed teachers, administrators, and shepherds by the Spirit....

"I invite you to join me as active partners in the Church's evangelizing mission. Together may we humbly open our minds and hearts to the Spirit. May we use the many talents and gifts God has given us to proclaim the Good News; to make Jesus known and loved...."[5]

*Pope John Paul II* on December 11, 1979, met with 13 leaders of the Catholic charismatic renewal representing the Council of the International Communications Office (ICO). Concerning the charismatic renewal, the Pope said, "I am convinced that this movement is a very important component of the entire renewal of the Church."

Pope John Paul II told the group that since he was 12 or 13 years old, he has daily said a prayer to the Holy Spirit in a prayer book his father gave him.

"This was my own spiritual initiation, so I can understand all these different charisms. They are all part of the richness of the Lord. I am convinced that this movement is a sign of his action," the Pope said, speaking of the charismatic renewal.

The informal 90-minute meeting began with the watching of a 40-minute television program which gave an overview of the 13-year history of the Catholic charismatic renewal. The program was produced especially for this presentation by members of the Community of God's Delight, Dallas, Texas, with help from some 100 other groups and individuals throughout the world.

At the end of the program, the Pope clapped in appreciation. "Thank you. It was an expression of the faith," he said.

Six reports on various aspects of the charismatic renewal were then given. Two persons spoke about renewal in Latin America. There was a report on street evangelization in Paris, France, and on the evangelistic capabilities of television. Father Forrest spoke about how the charismatic renewal was enabling thousands of priests to overcome loneliness and weakness by receiving God's loving power.

Ralph Martin, of Brussels, the former ICO director, gave a report on the growth and spread of charismatic communities and on the formation of an international association of communities. Following his presentation, Martin gave a moving statement of the loyalty of charismatics to the Pope.[6]

## The Fruits of the Spirit's Action in the Charismatic Renewal:

The fruits of this sovereign action of the Spirit can be seen in the lives of those baptized in the Holy Spirit. They *experience* the basic Gospel message. They experience *Jesus as Savior and Lord in a personal way,* believe in him with expectant faith and turn to him in ongoing conversion. They also experience the *power of the Holy Spirit,* are possessed by him, guided by him, used by him through such gifts as prophecy and healing, and enjoy his presence as they worship in various forms of prayer. Finally, they experience the *Lordship of Jesus in a communal way,* submitting to him and to one another in loving Christian community.

The Spirit has brought us far, but there is more—so very much more, as the Spirit himself began to show the national leaders of the Catholic charismatic renewal in August, 1978.

## NOTES

1. This account is taken from Fr. Val Gaudet, O.M.I., **"A Woman and the Pope,"** New Covenant, October, 1973.
2. **Humanae Salutis,** Second Vatican Council, December 25, 1961.
3. Early works on the Catholic Pentecostal (Charismatic) renewal: Kevin and Dorothy Ranaghan, **Catholic Pentecostals,** 1969, Paulist Press, New York, N.Y.; Rev. Edward O'Connor, **The Pentecostal Movement in the Catholic Church,** 1971, Ave Maria Press, Notre Dame, IN 46556.
4. **New Covenant,** July, 1975.
5. Archbishop J. L. Bernardin, **"The Charismatic Movement—A Gift to the Living Church,"** New Covenant, August 1976.
6. Taken from Kevin Ranaghan, **"Appointment in Rome,"** New Covenant, March, 1980.

# Chapter II

# Why Has the Charismatic Renewal Peaked?

In August of 1978 at the Advisory Committee meeting at South Bend, Indiana, national leaders of the Catholic charismatic renewal became aware of a peaking in the renewal in the areas of decreased attendance at conferences and prayer meetings and fewer sales of books. What is the cause for this so-called peaking phenomenon? Could it not be that the charismatic renewal has peaked because it is a "peak experience"? The very nature of a mountaintop experience is that it is followed by a descent from the mountain.

We believe that the charismatic renewal is a mountaintop experience with a very definite purpose and value, namely, to prepare for the coming down from the mountain to face the difficult times ahead.[1]

## The Charismatic Renewal as a Tabor Experience

The transfiguration of Jesus on Mount Tabor can be considered as a "sneak preview" of the glory to come. Tabor itself was a prediction of the descent from the mountaintop to the valley of spiritual warfare leading to the ultimate battle on the cross and to the resurrection.

The event of the transfiguration is set within a series of charismatic events in the life of Jesus. The

11

sequence of these events in all three of the synoptic Gospels shows this (e.g., Matthew 15-17): Jesus' healings of the suffering and feeding of the four thousand, the profession of Peter, the first prophecy of the passion and resurrection, the teaching on the doctrine of the cross, Jesus' transfiguration, the deliverance of the possessed boy and the second prophecy of the passion. In Luke's account of the transfiguration (Luke 9:31), Jesus speaks with Moses and Elijah of his coming passion.

The same pattern of events is true for the charismatic renewal. Using the principle that what has happened to the Head, Jesus, is to happen to his Body, the Church, what we see happening is the descent from Tabor in order to ascend Calvary. The charismatic renewal has been a Tabor experience of glory for a time, as a *sneak preview* of the glory that is to come after the crucifixion and resurrection.

In *praying* for a new Pentecost we must realize that we have not yet experienced the full reality, only the sneak preview. We must still pass through the travail of a corporate Calvary in the body of Christ in order to bring the salvation of Christ Jesus to all the nations.

In *experiencing* our Tabor we have also experienced the events that surrounded the transfiguration: the profession of Jesus as Lord, the healings, the deliverances, the miracles, the prophecies, the teachings, in short, the glory of transfiguration.

*But* the charismatic renewal must not misunderstand this experience as Peter did. After professing Jesus as the Messiah (Matthew 16:16) Peter immediately misinterpreted the nature of the Messiah and was reprimanded by the Lord (Matthew 16:22). And again Peter misinterpreted the meaning of the transfiguration and wanted to stay on top of the mountain. "Lord, it is good that we are here! With your permission I will erect three booths, one for you, one for Moses, and one for Elijah'' (Matthew 17:4). The charismatic renewal, like Peter, must learn that it is necessary for the Son of Man to suffer and die and so enter into his glory (see Luke 24:26 and 46).

As the Head, so the Body!

## The Missing Elements of Tabor

Tabor was only a preview of what was to come and did not include two essential elements in the plan of the Father before Pentecost could occur: the *Hour* of our Lord's passion and the presence of his mother *Mary*. Tabor was not *the* Hour and Mary was not on Tabor. But at the Hour of Calvary Mary was there and was explicitly commissioned in the last command of Jesus to be mother of the disciples of Jesus. She was commissioned by Jesus to do for his Body the Church what she had done for him as Head of the Church. And we in the person of the beloved disciple, John, were commissioned to take Mary as our own.

## The Lesson of John the Beloved Disciple

Peter along with James and his brother John, the beloved disciple, were with Jesus on Tabor and they saw his glory (Matthew 17:1-2). These three disciples are something like the members of the charismatic renewal in that they, unlike the rest of the disciples, were given a foretaste of the glory of Jesus. Because of this privilege the three disciples had a special responsibility to remember the lesson of Tabor in the days of trial ahead and to strengthen their brethren.

Of the three, only John, the beloved disciple, remembered. True, he fled from the garden of Gethsemane, but then he remembered the lesson of Tabor and returned to the cross. There, he stood with

Mary, the mother of Jesus (John 19:25-27). There at the command of Jesus, he received the mother of Jesus and took her as his own.

In a powerful scriptural teaching on Mary given to some one thousand priests at the National Conference for Priests on the Charismatic Renewal held at the College of Steubenville in 1978, Father Francis Martin explained the meaning of the phrase, "the disciple took her into his care (or home)." He said that this passage does indeed mean what it literally says but that it also means much more. It applies to all of us disciples and means that we should welcome Mary as our own and accept her as our spiritual heritage. It means that we must welcome Mary into the spiritual space within us constituted by communion with Jesus. This demands faith and is an ecclesial experience. [2]

This description by Father Martin is also a description of consecration to Mary in which we entrust our whole lives to Mary, the mother of Jesus, as our mother.

As a result of his consecration to Mary, John was empowered by her maternal intercession to stand with her through the crushing experience of the death of Jesus. And later in the Cenacle after Jesus had ascended to the Father, it was the inspiration and power of her intercession that enabled the beloved disciple to pray with expectant faith for the "promise of the Father" and to experience the full glory of Pentecost.

Now we, like John the beloved disciple, are being called to this spiritual heritage. But we are being called to entrust ourselves to the mother of Jesus even *before* the full experience of Calvary so that she can prepare our hearts for the travail.

As we begin our ascent of Calvary we must entrust ourselves to Mary. This is the final secret of the Lord's plan for the renewal of his Church.

15

## NOTES

1. See G. W. Kosicki, **The Mountaintop Experience: Its Value and Purpose in Spiritual Growth, Review for Religious**, 35, 1976.
2. Francis Martin, **Living in the Vision,** #78 PC11, Conference Cassettes, P. O. Box 8617, Ann Arbor, MI 48107.

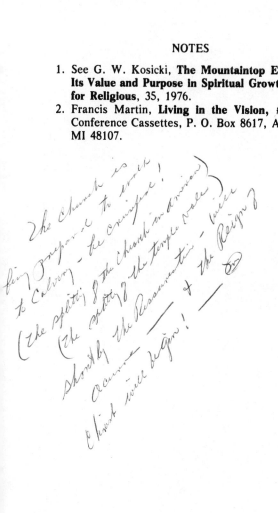

# Chapter III

# When and Where Did the Charismatic Renewal Peak?

In our view the charismatic renewal had it greatest Tabor experience on Pentecost Sunday, May 18, 1975, during the Holy Year, as Pope Paul VI celebrated the Eucharist in St. Peter's Basilica in Rome for ten thousand people gathered for the International Conference on the Charismatic Renewal in the Catholic Church and for thousands more gathered at that same time for the International Mariological and Marian Congress as well as for many thousands of other pilgrims who filled the Basilica.

This event was the pinnacle of the mountain top experience characterizing the charismatic renewal. Here was a moment of glory for the Church that was a sneak preview of what is to come for the whole Church. This Pentecost weekend was one of the great highlights of the Holy Year which was focused on Reconciliation and Renewal; it was a highlight for the Holy Father himself and a turning point in his attitude toward the charismatic renewal. It was during this weekend conference that the Church saw and heard the enthusiasm of the Holy Spirit expressed in the hearts of the faithful: in praise, in song, in dance and arms raised in prayer. It saw and heard the power of the Holy Spirit in healings, teachings and prophecy. It heard its chief shepherd proclaim with enthusiasm, "Jesus is Lord!"

This moment was the fulfillment of a dream that Cardinal Suenens had shared with the National Service Committee of the Catholic Charismatic Renewal. He had dreamed of a united international meeting of the Marian and Mariological Society and the Charismatic Conference in St. Peter's Basilica with the Holy Father presiding. Cardinal Suenens then shared this dream in a pictorial way at the charismatic conference held at the University of Notre Dame, June, 1974, when he said prophetically that if the charismatic renewal was to fly over the whole world, it would have to be empowered by the Spirit and borne on two wings, one being Mary, the Mother of the Church and the other, Peter, the visible head of the Church. In the Basilica of St. Peter on Pentecost Sunday this prophecy was symbolically fulfilled. We see this symbolic event as calling all in the charismatic renewal to an intimate union with Mary and Peter. We see it also as a reminder to us of the prayer of Pope John XXIII for a new Pentecost in which he prayed prophetically, "...grant that your Church, praying perseveringly and insistently with one heart and mind *together with Mary,* the Mother of Jesus, and *guided by blessed Peter,* may increase the reign of the Divine Savior...." This event in Rome was not the new Pentecost, but a Tabor event, prefiguring the full reality of a new Pentecost.

To experience the full reality of the new Pentecost, the Church and so the charismatic renewal has to descend from Tabor, descend from its moment of glory in order to ascend Calvary. Calvary is the necessary "passage" of which Jesus spoke to Moses and Elijah while on Tabor (Luke 9,31) and of which he spoke to his disciples (Luke 9:43-45; 24:25-27). It is the "passage" that must come before the resurrection and Pentecost.

The next day, from the podium of the high altar of St. Peter's Basilica, several prophecies were given preparing the people for total reliance on the Lord in time of darkness to come upon the world and a time of glory for the Church. This was a word preparing the people for spiritual combat, for great evangelization, for a new day of victory and triumph for the Lord and his Church.[2] This word was the beginning of the descent from Tabor as it spoke of the time ahead as one of change, combat and trial. It was like Jesus' speaking of his coming passion and death with his disciples as he descended from the mountain.

This peak experience of Pentecost Sunday, 1975, was a necessary and valuable one. It gave us a vision that must be kept alive as we descend from Tabor and ascend Calvary. The charismatic renewal has a real and necessary mission in and for the Church. It must keep alive the vision of the new Pentecost. Having itself experienced this in a moment of glory, it must continue to remind the Church of what is in store for it as it is surrounded by an ever growing darkness in the world. Its mission is specifically to encourage the people of God not to forget, to strengthen their weak knees and to persevere on their journey (Heb. 12:1-12).

In the ascent of Calvary the charismatic renewal and all the people of God will need to be strengthened and sustained by our Mother Mary. Mary was the first gift Jesus gave us on the Cross (John 19:27). Only after giving us Mary as our mother did Jesus "deliver over his spirit" (John 19:30), a phrase that Father Francis Martin says indicates the pouring forth of the Holy Spirit.[3] And as his final gift from the Cross, there flowed from his pierced side blood and water (John 19:34), symbolizing, as the Church Fathers loved to point out, the new Eve, his Bride, in a word, all of us, the Church. Mary will prepare us for Calvary and prepare us to receive the Holy Spirit coming upon us in the new Pentecost. This "secret of Mary" was the

secret that Cardinal Suenens revealed to the
Charismatic Conference of 1973 at the University of
Notre Dame, adding, "It is a secret that you can tell
everyone!" This is a secret to be accepted, lived, and
proclaimed by the charismatic renewal.


## NOTES

1.  Rev. Edward O'Connor, **Pope Paul and the Spirit,**
    1978, Ave Maria Press, p. 54.
2.  **New Covenant,** July, 1975.
3.  National Conference for Priests on the Charismatic
    Renewal 1978, College of Steubenville, Tape #78,
    PC11 available from Conference Cassettes, P.O.
    Box 8617, Ann Arbor, MI 48107.

# Chapter IV

# Visions of Renewal

Two visions of what God is doing to renew his Church through the charismatic renewal stand out among others. One vision is the prophetic teaching of Ralph Martin called *God is Restoring His People* in which he described three converging rivers within the Pentecostal renewal. The second is the prophetic vision of Derek Prince in which he saw the Pentecostal movement as a wave receding to make place for *a greater and final wave* following it. Both these visions portray a new and greater future for the Church, but both visions lack details in regard to the future. Neither gives an insight on *how* the plan of God will be achieved.

It is precisely in these areas of the nature of the future Church and the *how* of the achievement that the specifically Catholic elements of our Church bring a wealth of insight.

## The Three Converging Rivers

On Sunday, June 16, 1974, Ralph Martin addressed the International Conference on the Catholic Charismatic Renewal. Thirty thousand people were gathered that day in the football stadium of the University of Notre Dame, South Bend, Indiana. It was a cold and rainy day, but the message was anointed. Interrupted more than 20 times by applause, Ralph Martin's talk was prophetic and set a new direction for the charismatic renewal. "We are moving from an apologetic phase to a prophetic phase," he said and went on to describe the situation within the Church today. He continued, "Renewal is too weak a word for what needs to happen in the Christian Church. 'Renewal' can give us a sense that we will just polish something up a bit. Rather, I think God is moving to *restore* New Testament Christianity to all his people and that is more than renewal." He pictured the Pentecostal renewal taking place in the Church as three rivers: the classic Pentecostal River (1900- ), the neo-Pentecostal River (1957), and the Catholic Pentecostal River (1967- ). "I believe that in a very deep way God is moving to change the course of these mighty rivers. They have been flowing separately, but God is working on the riverbeds to enable them to flow together, to present a united witness to the Church and world. I don't know *how* God is going to do it, and I don't know when, but I know he's begun and he'll complete it. . . . What we're experiencing in the Holy Spirit is not something private or personal, just for us; it's something that's cosmic in scope. What's unfolding is a mighty plan from God."[1]

This "Three Rivers" talk of Ralph Martin had a profound effect on the leaders of the Catholic charismatic renewal as expressed by the Advisory Committee that met afterwards to evaluate the conference.[2] This talk provided the key impetus for convoking the ecumenical conference on the charismatic renewal at Kansas City, July, 1977, for over 50,000 people.

What we have seen in the charismatic renewal of the Church so far has been primarily an influx of new experiences and teachings from the classic Pentecostals on such things as the baptism in the Holy Spirit, tongues, prophecy, healings and other ministerial gifts of the Holy Spirit. From the neo-Pentecostal churches has come the thrust toward renewal of parishes and local communities. From the Catholic Church have come experience and teaching on order and community as seen in the development of covenant communities. But the *specifically* Catholic elements have not yet entered into the main thrust of the river, namely, the Church as *Church,* with its three basic elements: the Eucharist, Mary and the Pope. These three elements are what makes the Church truly an incarnate Church, that is, a Church enfleshed by Mary through the Holy Spirit, fed by the Risen Body of the Lord in the Eucharist and united under the visible vicar of Christ, the Pope.

In his talk Ralph Martin states that he doesn't know *how* or *when* God is going to bring these rivers together. We believe that the *how* of this mighty work is being revealed through the Catholic river. Many revelations coming from within the Catholic river such as the revelations given to the children at Fatima in 1917 and continuing during subsequent years, as well as private revelations to Father Stefano Gobbi (of which we will speak in Chapter VI) among others, speak of the specific role of Mary in God's plan for a cosmic renewal of the Church. The *how* of this new phase of renewal must involve Mary as mother. As she was mother of Jesus, the Head, so she is mother of his Body, the Church.

## A Greater and Final Wave

In the issue of *New Covenant* which carried Ralph Martin's address Derek Prince[3] too shared a prophetic vision of the renewal of the Church. In October, 1964, Derek was overlooking the sea from a clifftop when the

24

Lord showed him that the history of the Church was like the behavior of the sea: high tides, low tides and a series of ever-renewing waves. Derek goes on to relate:

"The Pentecostal movement had been one of the great waves. It had recovered truth not recovered by previous waves, and had made an impact all around the earth. But it had reached its climax and was receding. That was almost a physical blow. I thought, 'God, am I giving my life to something that's on the way out? What am I to do?'...This is the answer the Lord gave me: 'The same wave never comes back again, but some of the water that is in the previous wave comes back in the next one.' There's a new wave coming; it will not be the *Pentecostal* movement; it will be different. It will come higher even than the Pentecostal movement; *it will recover truth which Pentecostals as a whole did not recover*. It will be the greatest wave and it will be the last wave."

Here is a striking description of the phenomenon of peaking in the charismatic renewal; it is a peaking which prepares for the next wave. This next wave will be different; it will be the greatest and last wave. This is a good description of the Catholic wave that is coming and will usher in the glorious reign of Christ. The Marian aspect of this wave is looked at more closely in Part II where we consider specifically the role of Mary in the new Pentecost.

If we reflect on and understand the purpose of the charismatic renewal, we will appreciate that it is a preparation for something greater. That there is something greater coming is also the message of the Marian revelations.

## NOTES

1. **New Covenant,** September, 1974.
2. See the compiled remarks in **"A Prophetic Vision,"** **New Covenant,** September, 1974.
3. Derek Prince is an internationally-known author and speaker who has been in full time Pentecostal ministry for over thirty years.

Jan 1985
I was told -
"I am holding you in
abeyance - for there is
worse things to come"
Sam

**Chapter V**

# Prophecies of Renewal

There is a selection of prophetic words recorded in the July 1975, *New Covenant,* giving five of the so-called "Rome prophecies", that is, prophecies given at St. Peter's Basilica during the closing Eucharist on the day after Pentecost, May 19, 1975. These and other prophecies given on other occasions including the 1977 Conference on Charismatic Renewal in the Christian Churches, held at Kansas City are recorded in the February, 1978, *New Covenant* where Bruce Yocum and Kevin Ranaghan comment on the significance of these prophecies.

These prophecies speak of a tribulation coming for the world by a time of glory for the Church. They are a call to be prepared for the times ahead.

These prophecies have had a significant impact on the vision of the charismatic renewal. They have affected the pattern of thinking and acting of many charismatic leaders and communities. The association of covenant communities, for example, have banded together in order to give support to each other and to those who seek their help, in the "days of darkness" that lie ahead.

For some, these prophecies have been a source of support but for others a cause of division. Some have dismissed them as mere "doomsday" prophecies.

Others have said "yes, this is a powerful word" but have not acted upon the word. Still others within the Catholic Church have heard the word but are waiting for the hierarchy to discern it. Finally, some have heard this word and have changed their attitudes and their life-style because of it. With this last group we consider that these prophecies are a genuine word of the Lord spoken to us in our present situation and, as such, should be responded to by a change in our attitudes and activities.[1]

We also believe that the Lord speaks to us in many ways and that these prophecies do not reveal the whole of the Lord's plan for the renewal of his Church. With this in mind we want to look at these prophecies in the light of other revelations concerning the renewal of the Church.

We believe that the content of these prophecies can be summarized in the following words:

"Because I love you, I want to prepare you for what is coming: a time of darkness and tribulation for the world which will also be a time of testing and purification for the Church, preparing it for a new age, a time of glory and a time of great evangelization. I will be with you, preparing you to rely on me, preparing you for spiritual combat in which you will need a new wisdom, a new power and a new understanding. You will have all the gifts of the Holy Spirit. But I ask you to repent, to turn away from the values of the world, to band together, to be followers of my true shepherds and to be ready to lay down your lives. I ask you, further, to lament and intercede because of the desperation of these times, because the Body of my Son is broken and some of my shepherds are not the shepherds I want them to be."

To these prophecies, we believe should be added three other sources which have spoken clearly and powerfully to us of the times ahead: recent papal statements, the revelations of Fatima, and the message of a book entitled *Our Lady Speaks to Her Beloved Priests* (See Chapter VI).

The statements of Pope Paul VI and Pope John Paul II have developed each of the points made in these prophecies.[2] Also, the message of our Lady given at Fatima and subsequent locutions to Sister Lucy bring out each point made in these prophecies. The Fatima message has the added force of papal recognition.[3] And in the greatest detail the words of *Our Lady Speaks to Her Beloved Priests* develop each point made in these prophecies.

But in addition to the confirmation given to these prophecies by these sources there is a major common feature that goes beyond them. Each of these sources adds the specifically *Catholic* elements of our Catholic Church: the Eucharist, Mary, and the Pope in union with the bishops. We believe that the role of these Catholic elements is called for in the following prophecies:

"You need *wisdom* from me that you do not have. You need the *power* of my Holy Spirit in a way that you have not possessed it; You need *understanding* of my will and of the ways that I work that you do not yet have."[4]

It is our conviction that *Mary* is to provide the new wisdom and new power that we do not yet have in order to understand the ways of the Lord and to accomplish his work.

Mary is the chosen vessel of God who not only cooperated with the Holy Spirit to bring forth Christ, but has been chosen to continue this cooperation by bringing his Body, the Church, into the glorious reign of the new Pentecost.

30

## NOTES

1. See G. W. Kosicki, **"Preparing for Difficult Times,"** **New Covenant,** August, 1978.
2. G. W. Kosicki, **Pilgrimage and Purification: The Church in Travail in the '80's,** 1980, Crux, 75 Champlain St., Albany, NY 12204.
3. For example, J. M. Alonso, **The Secret of Fatima,** 1979, The Ravengate Press, Cambridge, MA 02138. (Available from AMI Press, Washington, NJ 07882.)
4. Rome, May 19, 1975, see **New Covenant,** July, 1975.

# Part Two

# The Bride Says,
# "Come!"

In Part II, we describe what we believe to be in God's plan the indispensable role of Mary in preparing the Bride, the Church, to cry out with the Spirit, "Come, Lord Jesus. Come and reign in a new Pentecost."

In our introduction we pointed out two occasions when the Spirit has invited the Bride to join him in such a cry. On the first occasion the invitation extended through Pope Leo XIII received an inadequate response from the Bride. On the second occasion the invitation extended through Pope John XXIII has not yet received a full response from the Bride. We pointed out that the Catholic charismatic renewal has provided the Bride with a *"sneak preview"* of the new Pentecost. But much more is needed. The bride, that is, the whole Church, must cry out together with the Spirit, "Come!" To do this she must be purified on Calvary. In this purification Mary will be not only the model of what the Bride is to become, but also the mother, guiding the Church with her maternal care through Calvary to the Cenacle in preparation for the new Pentecost.

In Part I, we pointed out the problem in the charismatic renewal of the Church and indicated that the answer lies in Mary. In Part II, we want to develop the role of Mary in the renewal of the Church, beginning with the account of how we came to this answer ourselves. The most influential factor in our coming to this answer was our acceptance of the message of the Marian Movement of Priests as a prophetic word to the Church in our time, and so we begin Part II by looking at this movement.

Chapter VI

# The
# Marian Movement
# of Priests

The Marian Movement of Priests has been the basic inspiration for the Marian insights shared in these teachings. The purpose of this movement is to prepare priests for the time of travail in the Church.

It is based on a series of private revelations given by our Blessed Mother to Father Stefano Gobbi of Milan, Italy. These are recorded in a diary beginning in July, 1973, called *Our Lady Speaks to Her Beloved Priests.*[1] As private revelations they have required and received our careful discernment.

The director of the Marian Movement of Priests in the United States, Father Albert Roux, points out:

"In this book Mary has a very beautiful and inspiring message for all of us. Although she speaks of the difficulties and purification awaiting the Church and the world, she brings us a message of hope as she speaks of her great victory to come. 'My victory has already begun, and soon it will blaze forth over all the Church and over the whole of renewed humanity...' (Dec. 8, 1975). The late Pope Paul, to whom a copy of this book had been given, encouraged and blessed on three different occasions Fr. Stefano Gobbi, the recipient of the messages of Our Lady and the founder of the Marian Movement of Priests."[2]

33

The content of *Our Lady Speaks to Her Beloved Priests* as well as the response to it received from thousands of priests and bishops around the world speaks for its authenticity. Our own response to it is an ever increasing "yes" as we daily reread and ponder its message.

This message of Our Lady could be considered a continuation of the message given to the children of Fatima, addressed now to priests. Our Lady reveals a plan to renew the Church through her priests. She calls for a consecration of priests to her Immaculate Heart, priests who will be taught by her how to be an army of little ones that will overcome the work of sin and the Evil One. Here, by way of example, is a message dated March 9, 1979, taken from the 6th edition:

"Beloved sons, consider with me the signs of the times in which you are living. The hearts of men have become cold, and the entire world has become a desert.

"But more than ever you should have confidence in your heavenly Mother! Look, with me, at the times in which you are living, and you will see the indications of my extraordinary intervention.

"When the first buds appear upon the trees, you say winter is now drawing to an end and that a new spring is approaching.

"I have pointed out to you the signs of the cruel winter through which the Church is passing in the purification which has become most painful.

"The Spouse of my Jesus still appears covered with wounds and darkened by her adversary who seems to be in the process of celebrating a total victory.

"He is convinced that he has won the victory

within the Church by the confusion which has corrupted so many of her truths, by the lack of discipline which has sown discord, by insubordination which has affected her interior unity, by an insidious and hidden persecution which has crucified her anew.

"But see how, in her worst winter, the buds of a renewed life are beginning to appear. They tell you that the hour of your liberation is near.

"For the Church, a new springtime of the triumph of my Immaculate Heart, is about to be born. She will still be the same Church, but a Church renewed, illumined, made humbler, stronger, poorer, more evangelical by its purification, in order that she may make resplendent for all, the glorious reign of my Son, Jesus.

"This will be the new Church of Light, and already many new buds may be seen sprouting on her branches: these are all those who have had confidence in their heavenly Mother—you, Apostles of my Immaculate Heart.

"You are these buds, my little children, who are consecrated to me and who live by my own spirit.

"You are these buds, faithful disciples of Jesus, who are desirous of living a life of contempt for the world and for yourselves, in poverty, in humility, in silence, in prayer and mortification, in charity, in union with God, while at the same time you are unknown and scorned by the world.

"The time has arrived to come forth from the shadows in order to go and enlighten the world. Present yourselves to everyone as my sons, for I am always with you. Let faith be the light that enlightens you in these days of darkness, and may you be consumed only by zeal for the honor and glory of God.

"Carry on the combat, sons of Light, even though you are still few in number! Many will follow in your footsteps and will become part of my cohort, because the hour for my battle has arrived.

"In this hardest of winters, it is you, my little ones, who are the buds that burgeon forth from my Immaculate Heart and which I place on the branches of the Church to indicate to you that her most beautiful springtime is at hand.

"It will be like a new Pentecost for the Church."

The message we have just quoted reveals something of great importance to the whole Church. Mary tells us that the triumph of her Immaculate Heart is identical with the new Pentecost for the Church. In doing so she indicates that the new Pentecost prayed for by Pope John XXIII is soon to be experienced by us. Why? Because repeatedly in the messages of this book Our Lady assures us that in the near future we shall see the complete triumph of her Immaculate Heart. She is thus telling us that the words she spoke to the children of Fatima on July 13, 1917, "...in the end my Immaculate Heart will triumph," are soon to be fulfilled.

In Chapter VIII we shall explain why the triumph of the Immaculate Heart of Mary and the triumph of the Holy Spirit in the new Pentecost are one and the same. As an essential condition for this triumph Our Lady calls for a consecration to her Immaculate Heart, which is to be lived out by exterior and interior docility. This docility means obedience to the Gospel, to Jesus, and to the vicar of Christ on earth and the bishops in union with him. To live out this consecration means to suffer because of love, to be silent as we listen, and to pray, especially using the rosary which she has given us and wants us to pray daily.[3] To live out this consecration means to live in the Immaculate Heart of our Mother and be led to an ever greater docility.

In a circular letter of September 15, 1979, Father Stefano Gobbi capsulized the spirituality of the movement: "A priest from Ireland once observed that the book is almost a carbon copy of the de Montfort Consecration, a retelling of the doctrine of the child-like spirituality of Saint Therese of the Child of Jesus, and the actuality of the message of Fatima."

We would add that the Marian Movement includes the important element of community by encouraging the formation of Cenacles, that is, informal groups of two or more priests gathered about Mary in prayer and fraternal love, just as in the original Cenacle. It also provides for lay associates who consecrate themselves to Mary and support the priests of the Movement by their prayers, works and sufferings. They too are encouraged to form Cenacles.

This message of Our Lady has the greatest urgency about it. It is a message of deep compassion for the Church and its priests. In its clarity and calling, it moves beyond the prophetic messages given in Rome in May, 1975, and Kansas City in July, 1977. The whole thrust of the message is to prepare the priests, and so the people of God, for the time of travail upon us.

### NOTES

1. English translation, P.O. Box 8, St. Francis, ME 04774.
2. Letter with the 4th Edition of the text.
3. In each of the six apparitions at Fatima during 1917, Our Lady urged the daily praying of the Rosary.

**Chapter VII**

# God's Plan for Mary
# in the New Pentecost

To begin these reflections on Mary in the new Pentecost we might well ask, "*What* is God's plan for the new Pentecost and *how* does he want to accomplish it?"

The best way to learn the answer is to let God tell us, and in fact God has spoken to us through a variety of ways: sacred scripture, the teachings of the Church and private revelations. In the last century and a half, for example, he has spoken to us through a variety of Marian revelations. It is in this area that the Church plays an essential role in the discernment of spirits. She is to discern whether these revelations can be safely believed in. In fact over the last century and a half the Church has approved at least twelve series of Marian revelations and messages. Some of the messages have the recognition of the local diocese and others, such as the revelations of Fatima, have been confirmed by the response of Pope Pius XII and by the presence of Pope Paul VI at Fatima as well as his consecration of the world to Mary at the end of the third session of the Second Vatican Council.

It is important to hear what the Lord is saying through these messages if we want to know the "what" and "how" of God's plan for a new Pentecost. The Catholic charismatic renewal, for example, is familiar with prophecy and its discernment, but not all in the renewal are familiar with messages that come through Mary. There is a predisposition to hear these words because they are like prophecies, but there is also among some a predisposition not to hear them because of a lack of expectant faith in Mary's speaking to us as her children.

The Marian messages and the role of Mary in God's plan have been a problem for some in the charismatic renewal because of ecumenical sensitivity. In the past the charismatic renewal has had to face up to difficult questions that caused divisions and misunder-standings. In the early days of the charismatic renewal the concern was over the nature of the baptism in the Holy Spirit and the place of the gift of tongues. Later the issue was the deliverance and healing ministry, and then prophecy. A serious issue developed when prayer groups moved into covenant communities. All these issues led to purification and growth. Now the Catholic charismatic renewal has to face the issue of Mary's role in the new Pentecost, and this is an issue not only for those in the charismatic renewal, but for the entire Church.

With this in mind let us return to the basic questions concerning God's plan for a new Pentecost. We will consider these questions in light of Marian revelations that have been confirmed by the Church.

### What is God's Plan for a New Pentecost?

God is preparing the Church, his Bride, by purifying her (Eph. 5:26). This work is yet to be completed. Its completion will be the new Pentecost prayed for by John XXIII. It will bring about the reign of Jesus as Lord in a glorious Church. Our understanding of this reign has been enriched by prayerful study of Scripture and of Marian revelations. It may be summarized thus:

* To complete his plan, Jesus is to return in order to reign with his purified and trans- figured Bride, the Church.
* This coming of Jesus is not his final coming, but it is his coming in glory to reign in the hearts of the faithful.
* It will be a reign of resplendence with the light of Christ shining in the hearts of all believers.
* It will be a renewed Church of Light, a Light that will bring salvation to all the nations.

### How Does God Want to Accomplish the Plan of His Coming?

*How* is Christ preparing his Bride, the Church, for this glorious reign? In the same way that he himself was prepared, namely, by his being formed in the womb of Mary and being born of her, and by his life, passion, death and resurrection. Now his Church, mothered by Mary, is passing through the way of his passion as a purification and is thus being made ready for its reign with Christ. Like the first coming through Mary *and* the power of the Holy Spirit this coming will be through Mary and the Holy Spirit. It is a simple plan, and the simplicity of a child is needed to accept it.

The specific strategy for the victory of the Church over the Prince of Darkness is consecration to the Immaculate Heart of Mary. This strategy is essential to the message of Fatima and to the message of the Marian Movement of Priests. To inspire our acceptance of this strategy we have the stirring example of Pope John Paul II who has given himself in total consecration to Mary from the day of his ordination and has frequently renewed this consecration of himself and the

Church: in Rome, Mexico, Poland, Loreto, Ireland and Washington, D. C.

## No Longer a Hidden Plan

This is not a new plan. This is the way the Lord has chosen to work from the beginning. All through the centuries since his First Coming he has been coming through Mary to all Christians, even to those who are not aware of this, those to whom his plan is hidden. Now, however, God wants this plan made known and accepted by all. He wants Mary to be recognized as the Mediatrix of all his graces.[1]

Not only does God want his plan for Mary made known, but he has made it a condition for the new Pentecost. He wants his people and the nations to be consecrated to the Immaculate Heart of Mary in order that she prepare our hearts for his reign. Specifically he has chosen the consecration of Russia by the Pope in union with the bishops as a condition for the conversion of Russia (Fatima Revelations). This conversion will be a sign to the world of Mary's role in God's plan for bringing about the new Pentecost.

### NOTES

1. **Lumen Gentium,** #62, Second Vatican Council.

# Chapter VIII

# Mary, Model and Mother of the Bride

The two words "model and mother" summarize Mary's role in the new Pentecost. The Second Vatican Council in *Lumen Gentium*[1] described the role of Mary and the Church, using these two pivotal terms.

As *model* or prototype the Church can see in Mary what it is to be. "In the most holy Virgin the Church has already reached that perfection whereby she exists without spot or wrinkle."[2] And again in the *Constitution on the Sacred Liturgy* the document states that "In her (Mary) the Church upholds and admires the most excellent fruit of the redemption, and joyfully contemplates, as in a faultless model, that which she herself wholly desires and hopes to be."[3]

Mary is *model* of God's plan both in its conception and its heavenly fulfillment. She was "fashioned by the Holy Spirit into a kind of new substance and new creature, adorned from the first instant of her conception with the splendors of an entirely unique holiness."[4]

Mary is also *mother.* "In an utterly singular way she cooperated by her obedience, faith, hope and burning charity in the Savior's work of restoring supernatural life to souls. For this reason she is a mother to us in the order of grace....Taken up to heaven, she did not lay aside this saving role, but by her manifold acts of inter-

44

cession continues to win for us gifts of eternal salvation.... Therefore the Blessed Virgin is invoked by the Church under the titles of Advocate, Adjutrix and Mediatrix." [5] "The maternal duty of Mary toward men in no way obscures or diminishes (the) unique meditation of Christ, but rather shows its power." [6]

## Mary's Role as Mediatrix

Blessed Maximilian Kolbe, a pioneer in the field of modern Mariology, showed the unity of action between the Holy Spirit and the Blessed Mother and thus succeeded in making much clearer the how and why of Mary's universal mediation.

Father Manteau-Bonamy, commenting on Father Kolbe's Mariology, says:

"Father Kolbe shows clearly that the Most Blessed Virgin is not considered either as a mediatrix or a redeemer by herself....Intimately associated as she is with Christ's suffering and dying, the Virgin is, by the same Spirit, a true mediatrix in the sense which the Holy Spirit himself is a mediator (Rom. 8:26) with regard to the unique Mediator, Jesus Christ." [7] "...St. Paul realized perfectly well that if Jesus is indeed the one sole Mediator, the Holy Spirit himself is a Mediator between us and Christ....Because Mary is united to the Holy Spirit in such an ineffable manner, she takes part in this intimate mediation of the second Paraclete." [8]

A resume of Father Kolbe's thinking on the subject is found in a letter to one of his Brothers, who had inquired about the possibility of such mediation: "The union between the Immaculata and the Holy Spirit is so inexpressible, yet perfect, that the Holy Spirit acts only by the most Blessed Virgin, his Spouse. This is why she is Mediatrix of all grace given by the Holy Spirit."[9]

### Mary's "Saving Role"

Mary continues in her "saving role"[10] as our mother in heaven. She does so by cooperating in the redemption and salvation of all men by her continued union with her Son Jesus in his "yes" to the Father and by her preparation of the Church to do the same. The term "cooperative redemption" would be a more precise term than "co-redemption" to describe her role. The prefix "co-" in English implies an equality between the partners but in its Latin root "cum" means "with," so another term to describe Mary's role could be "redemption-with." Mary is a "redemptrix-with" the Lord Jesus. She was given the capacity to suffer with Jesus his passion and death. The prophecy of Simeon spoke of a sword piercing her heart (Luke 2:35). This close union continues in her saving role as she intercedes for us to win gifts of eternal salvation.[11]

What Mary is experiencing now as "redemptrix-with" the Lord Jesus is a foretaste of what the whole Church is to experience. The Church is to be the effective sign (sacrament) of salvation to the whole world.[12] What Mary is experiencing now as mother and model is the fulfillment and reality of what is in store for all of us! This "saving role" now exercised by Mary is to be *the* role of the Church in the world. The Church, like Jesus, the Head, is to ascend Calvary and shed its blood in union with him for the salvation of the world. Mary's role as mother is to prepare us for this "yes" on Calvary.

### Mary's Intimate Union with the Spirit

Mary's intimate union with the Holy Spirit is the *model* or prototype of the union of the Church and the

Spirit. It is fascinating to consider the intimacy of this union of Mary and the Spirit because this is what is in store for us as Purified Bride of Christ. The Church Fathers spoke of Mary as "spouse of the Holy Spirit;" the Second Vatican Council called her "the temple (sanctuary) of the Holy Spirit;"[13] Pope Paul VI described her as "the permanent dwelling of the Spirit of God."[14]

Blessed Maximilian Kolbe, in some very bold theological thinking, described the intimate relationship of Mary and the Holy Spirit in terms that are both startling and exciting. A few days before his arrest by the Nazis he wrote, "The Most Blessed Virgin is the one in whom we venerate the Holy Spirit, for she is his spouse. The third Person of the Blessed Trinity never took flesh; still, our human word 'spouse' is far too weak to express the reality of the relationship between the Immaculata and the Holy Spirit. We can affirm that she is, *in a certain sense,* the 'incarnation' of the Holy Spirit. It is the Holy Spirit that we love in her; and through her we love the Son."[15]

Father Manteau-Bonamy comments on this very carefully qualified statement: *"in a certain sense,* the 'incarnation' of the Holy Spirit," saying, "in reality there is no contradiction here. Between Mary the Immaculata and the Holy Spirit there is a deep union not only because Mary's will is absolutely conformed with that of the Holy Spirit, as a dutiful spouse's would be, and also because she was always a conscious and free instrument in his regard, a true handmaid but more precisely because the Holy Spirit dwells in her as in his privileged sanctuary."[16]

In his last writings, Father Kolbe wrote: "The Son is incarnate: Jesus Christ. The Holy Spirit is quasi-incarnate: the Immaculata."[17]

Another illustration of the intimate union between Mary and the Holy Spirit was given by Blessed

Maximilian Kolbe. He was fascinated by the phrase used by Mary during one of her apparitions to St. Bernadette at Lourdes, in France. In answer to St. Bernadette's question, "Who are you?" Mary replied, "I am the Immaculate Conception." This phrase was the source of a lifetime of reflection for Father Kolbe. He liked to point out that she did not say "I am the Immaculately Conceived," but rather said, "I *am* the Immaculate Conception." It was like saying, "I am whiteness" rather than saying, "I am white." Mary in describing herself as the Immaculate Conception described herself in terms that really apply to the Divinity itself. How could she apply this term to herself? Father Kolbe's insight was that at Lourdes Mary revealed an appropriate and meaningful name for the Holy Spirit himself. To explain this he wrote:

"And who is the Holy Spirit? The flowering of the love of the Father and the Son. If the fruit of created love is a created conception, then the fruit of divine Love, that prototype of all created love, is necessarily a divine 'conception.' The Holy Spirit is, therefore, the 'uncreated eternal conception,' the prototype of all the conceptions that multiply life throughout the whole universe.

"The Father begets; the Son is begotten; the Spirit is the 'conception' that springs from their love; there we have the intimate life of the three Persons by which they can be distinguished one from another. But they are united in the oneness of their nature, of their divine existence. The Spirit is, then, this thrice holy 'conception,' this infinitely holy 'immaculate conception'." [18]

So then, Mary as the Spouse of the Holy Spirit takes the name of her Spouse as her very own and can truly say of herself, "I am the Immaculate Conception." Father Kolbe put it this way in his final sketch: "If among human beings the wife takes the name of her husband because she belongs to him, is one with him, becomes equal to him, and is with him the source of new life, with how much greater reason should not the name of the Holy Spirit, who is the divine Immaculate Conception, be used as the name of her in whom he lives as uncreated Love, the principle of life in the whole supernatural order of grace?"[19]

It is because of this intimate union between the Holy Spirit and herself that Mary, in *Our Lady Speaks to Her Beloved Priests,* refers to the triumph of her Immaculate Heart as a new Pentecost.

The phrase describing Mary as the "quasi incarnation of the Holy Spirit" and the phrase used by Mary, "I am the Immaculate Conception," are phrases that also describe the union of the Church and the Holy Spirit. The Church is to be the visible manifestation of the Spirit's mission in the world. Through the power of the Holy Spirit the Church like Mary is to be the spotless Bride, mediating the redemption and salvation of Christ to all mankind. Or, as the Second Vatican Council said, the Church is to be the "Sacrament of intimate union with God and unity of all mankind."[20]

The mystery of the union of the Holy Spirit and the Bride of Christ is at the heart of the mystery of the Incarnation itself. Mary is the perfect prototype of what God wants for his Church, and she is also the mother chosen to bring forth this mystery of the Church by the power of the Holy Spirit. To emphasize this maternal role of his Spouse the Holy Spirit has often acted in a sovereign way through Mary down through the centuries of Christianity. Being the self-effacing Person of the Blessed Trinity who points out Jesus as Lord (1 Cor. 12:3) and God as Abba (Rom. 8:15), he also delights in pointing out Mary as mother (Luke 1:31; John 19:26) while keeping himself in the background. This he has done in a series of remarkable Marian revelations, some of which we will describe in the following chapter.

## NOTES

1.  **Lumen Gentium,** Chapter VIII, Second Vatican Council.
2.  **Lumen Gentium,** #65.
3.  **Sacrosanctum Concilium,** #103.
4.  **Lumen Gentium,** #56
5.  ibid #62.
6.  ibid #60.
7.  H.M. Manteau-Bonamy, **Immaculate Conception and the Holy Spirit: The Marian Teachings of Father Kolbe,** 1977, Prow Books, Kenosha, WI 53142, p. 96.
8.  ibid, p. 102.
9.  Letter to Father Mikolajczyk, July 28, 1935, quoted in ibid, p. 99.
10. **Lumen Gentium,** #62, Second Vatican Council.
11. ibid.
12. **Gaudium et Spes,** #45, Second Vatican Council.
13. **Lumen Gentium,** #53, Second Vatican Council.
14. **Marialis Cultis,** #26.
15. Conference, February 5, 1941, quoted in Manteau-Bonamy, ibid, p. 50.
16. ibid, p. 51.
17. February 17, 1941, quoted in ibid, p. 63.
18. February 17, 1941, ibid, p. 17.
19. ibid, p. 68.
20. **Lumen Gentium,** #1, Second Vatican Council.

# Chapter IX

# Sovereign Acts of the Holy Spirit through Mary

Catholics are familiar with three sovereign acts of the Holy Spirit performed through Mary last century in France. These were the apparitions at Rue du Bac, Paris, in 1830, resulting in the Miraculous Medal devotion, at LaSalette in 1846 and at Lourdes in 1858. These apparitions of Our Lady were all made to the *anawim*, the poor in spirit. In addition all three were the source of an outpouring of God's merciful love in the form of miraculous cures and, more important, of conversions to the Lord Jesus. Through these events God touched the lives of believers throughout the world, in the first event through the world-wide distribution and use of the Miraculous Medal, and in the other two events through pilgrimages of the faithful to the sites of Our Lady's apparitions.

## The Sovereign Act at Fatima [1]

Between the time of the Lourdes apparitions and today the most significant and well-known apparitions of Our Lady occurred in 1917 in Fatima, Portugal, again to the anawim. In the apparition of July 13, 1917, Mary revealed that her Son wishes to establish in the world devotion to her Immaculate Heart and that if this wish is complied with and Russia is consecrated to her

Immaculate Heart, Russia will be converted and there will be peace in the world. If not, she said, a second world war would break out during the pontificate of Pius XI, and Russia would spread her errors throughout the world, causing wars and persecutions of the Church. Later, in an apparition to Lucy on June 13, 1929, Our Lady made the request concerning the consecration of Russia more explicit, saying, "God asks the Holy Father, in union with all the bishops of the world, to make the consecration of Russia to my Immaculate Heart, promising to save it by this means."

As we know, these requests of God given by Mary were not complied with, and as a result many of the misfortunes foretold by Our Lady have already taken place. Nevertheless, the promise made by Our Lady at the end of the July, 1917, apparition still holds true: "But in the end my Immaculate Heart will triumph. The Holy Father will consecrate Russia to me, and it will be converted and some time of peace will be granted to humanity".

Our present Pope, as Cardinal of Cracow, joined all the Polish bishops in petitioning Pope Paul VI to make just such a consecration. And ever since his election as Pope he has repeatedly consecrated the Church to Mary at her shrines in various countries, and has strongly urged all the priests of the Church to follow his own example by consecrating themselves to Mary. Could it be that this is the man who will collegially consecrate Russia to the Immaculate Heart of Mary, bringing about its conversion and world peace? And could this consecration be an important, perhaps essential, step in bringing about the new Pentecost asked for by his predecessor John XXIII? We believe that the answer to both these questions is, "yes." We believe that the promise of Our Lady concerning the final triumph of her Immaculate Heart, the conversion of Russia, and the ensuing world peace is soon to be fulfilled. We say this knowing that not only is a collegial act of pope and bishops needed, but also that as a prerequisite *we ourselves*—individually and collectively—must consecrate ourselves to the Immaculate Heart of Mary. This is the core of the Fatima Message. This is God's will for us at this time in history concerning our relationship with Mary, his mother and ours.

As we ponder the message of Fatima, searching our hearts to determine our own response, we might do well to recall another apparition of Our Lady, one that took place on our own continent less than four decades after its discovery by Columbus. It, too, involved a sovereign act of the Holy Spirit through Mary bringing a veritable new Pentecost to an entire nation. It came about because the people to whom Mary spoke believed her message, accepted her fully as their mother, and allowed God to work his wonders through her intercession. This well-authenticated account provides an inspiring precedent for us, revealing how we must respond to Our Lady's message at Fatima.

## The Sovereign Act at Guadalupe [2]

On December 9, 1531, over four and a half centuries ago, a beautiful young woman surrounded by light as if standing in the sun appeared to a humble Aztec Indian named Juan Diego on a barren hilltop called Tepeyac just outside Mexico City. Speaking to him in his Indian language and cadence she told him that she was the "Immaculate Virgin Mary, Mother of the true God." She expressed her earnest desire that a church be built there and went on to tell him, "Here...I will give all my love, my compassion, my help and my protection to the people. I am your merciful mother, the merciful mother of all of you who live united in this land, and of all mankind, of all those who love me, of those who cry to me, of those who seek me, of those who have confidence in me. Here I will hear their weeping, their sorrows, and will remedy and alleviate their many sufferings...." She then asked him to go to the Bishop of Mexico City and tell him all that he had seen and heard.

Bishop Zumarraga was impressed with the humble sincerity of his Indian visitor, but as for his extraordinary tale about the beautiful young woman and her request for a church, well, that needed proof. And so he asked Juan Diego for a sign. Only three days later on December 12th he was given his sign. Earlier that morning the Virgin Mary had appeared once again to Juan Diego on the hillside path. As a sign for the Bishop she asked him to climb to the hilltop and cut the flowers that were growing there. Juan Diego knew that no flowers could bloom there in December; yet, he obeyed. To his amazement he found beautiful, fragrant roses, which he cut and brought to the young woman. She arranged them carefully in the fold of his mantle and told him to bring them to the Bishop. Without realizing it Juan Diego brought with him a far greater sign than the roses. For when he opened his mantle before the Bishop to display the roses, the astonished Bishop saw imprinted on the mantle the same image that had been imprinted on the vision of Juan Diego three days earlier, that of a young woman surrounded with sunlight. He saw and believed, and under his direction a simple adobe chapel built by both Indians and Spaniards was finished by Christmas Day. On the following day, the miraculous image was carried in joyful procession to the newly finished chapel and installed above the altar. Then, as the compassionate eyes of the mother looked upon her children, her Son was offered

for them to the Father in the Eucharistic Sacrifice.

From the beginning the Indians were drawn irresistably to the image. It had been given from heaven, and to one of their own race. At the Bishop's request Juan Diego took up residence in a room off the chapel and for the remaining seventeen years of his life recounted the apparitions and explained the meaning of the image to the visiting pagan Indians. Until the arrival of the Spanish ten years earlier, their written language had been a picture language; and so when they came to the adobe chapel they looked for a message in this image. On the day the Virgin had given her image to Juan Diego she also appeared in a final apparition to his uncle, Juan Bernardino, curing him miraculously of a serious disease and giving him a message for the Bishop. He was to tell the Bishop that her precious image would be named the Immaculate Virgin Mary and that it would crush the serpent. Juan Diego knew that the Indians worshipped a serpent god which they placated by offering thousands of human sacrifices annually. The Indian pictograph for this serpent was the crescent which the sacred image depicted beneath the feet of Our Lady. They also worshipped a sun god, and Juan Diego pointed out that the Virgin was blotting out the sun in this image. Clasped to her neck was a golden brooch with a small black cross; Juan Diego told them that Mary's Son had died on a cross to free them from bondage to false gods and make them children of a loving Father. It was clear that this woman was not herself a goddess for her hands were folded in prayer, prayer offered to her Son, the true God, for these, her children. It was easy to believe as they gazed at her that she was indeed a merciful mother who would alleviate their sufferings through her maternal intercession. And so they brought before her image their sick and pleaded with her for them; and her Son, who had borne their infirmities on the cross, healed them. All that the young woman had promised Juan Diego she fulfilled. News of the wonders God was working through his merciful mother spread like wildfire to all the Indians.

They in turn came to gaze upon the image and hear Juan Diego's words, and they too believed.

During the next seven years, 1532-1538, eight million Indians were converted to the Lord and were baptized! Missionaries were swamped with catechumens eager to hear their message. Illiterate Indians who could not be reached with the written word were able to grasp in the image of the compassionate young mother and in her words to Juan Diego the basic Gospel message: that God loved them, that he had sent his only Son Jesus to free them from the Evil One, from sin, and from sickness, that his Son was born of the Virgin Mary, and that Mary was their mother as well. And along with the basic Gospel message imprinted on Juan Diego's mantle were the many miraculous healings which they saw and experienced, healings worked through the intercession of the mother of mercy. The message Mary gave to these people through her words to Juan Diego, her miraculous image imprinted on his mantle, and the accompanying miracles opened their hearts; and the missionaries could now instruct the millions who came to them seeking baptism.

Eight million converts in seven years! What better description could be given to this event than to call it a new Pentecost? The message of Peter at Pentecost brought 3,000 converts to the faith. But if we divide the number of days in seven years into eight million converts we find that Mary's message brought an average of over 3,000 converts a day to the faith during a period of seven years—a new Pentecost every day for seven years!

And this event has proven to be a lasting one, both with regard to the miraculous image itself and to the effect that it has had on subsequent generations. Careful study of the mantle on which the image was imprinted reveals that it was woven from the fibers of a cactus plant and, as such, could last only thirty years. But to this day the image of the Virgin is just as fresh and beautiful as when Bishop Zumarraga first saw it four and a half centuries ago! God has miraculously preserved this fragile material during centuries of public display and handling. Not only has he preserved the material and its image, but he has preserved the presence of Mary there, on the hill of Tepeyac where she first appeared to Juan Diego, a presence mysterious and yet real, that is experienced and commented on by countless pilgrims to our Lady's image today, just as it has been over the centuries. And associated with this presence there has been a continuous outpouring of the Pentecostal signs of well authenticated miracles, healings, and new conversions to the Lord. The beautiful unity in the Spirit between Jew and Greek that was characteristic of Pentecost was matched by a truly remarkable unity between Indians and Spaniards brought about in a miraculous way. Ten years before Our Lady's apparitions Cortez had destroyed all the pagan idols of the Indians, leaving a religious void. Spanish misrule during the next ten years so antagonized the Indians that they were just at the point of exterminating the tiny band of foreigners when Our Lady's words and image brought them to the faith and with it to a firm and lasting unity with the Spaniards, bridging their many differences.

Over the centuries the little adobe chapel that first housed the sacred image grew in size to become a huge basilica. It is called the Basilica of Our Lady of Guada- lupe (a Spanish name which approximates the tongue-twisting Indian name Our Lady had given her image, meaning "it-will-crush-the-stone-serpent"). Here, throughout these past four centuries, marks of Pentecost have continuously been associated with the image: the apostolic instruction, the Christian communal life, the breaking of the Eucharistic bread, and the fervent prayers which reveal the deep faith of the Christians. As at Pentecost, the effect of the miraculous image of Guadalupe has been to establish the Lordship of Jesus Christ in the hearts of Mexicans and to keep it there.

From the beginning there has been an abundance of solid historical evidence for the Guadalupe event, and for over four centuries twenty-six popes, notably Benedict XIV and Leo XIII, have fostered the devotions founded on its apparitions. Clearly the discernment of our highest pastoral authority, the Holy See, is that the Blessed Virgin truly appeared at Guadalupe and that her image venerated there is miraculous.

If we examine the words our Lady of Guadalupe spoke to Juan Diego, we find that she did not confine her maternal intercession to the people of Mexico. When she said, "I am your merciful mother, the merciful mother of all of you who live united in this land", she stood squarely in the center of the New World, looking out on a vast hemisphere still to be divided into nations. It would be another two and a half centuries, for example, before our own United States would come into existence. She spoke, then, to us just as much as she spoke to the people of what is now Mexico. And her message and presence are needed by us in this time of deepening crisis in the Church and world just as much as they were needed in Mexico in 1531: those who are spiritually attuned to the needs of our time agree that only a sovereign act of God can meet our present needs, an outpouring of the Spirit such as occurred at Guadalupe.

### The Significance of Guadalupe

What, then, does the message of Guadalupe say to us Catholics of the United States and the world today? If we examine the sacred image we see that an angel, with wings spread as if ceasing from flight, is holding the hem of the garment worn by this visitor from heaven. The right foot of the Virgin is placed firmly on the crescent. The left foot is raised, indicating she is stepping forward. Forward into what? Into our hearts, if they are open to receive her. To do what? The cross on the brooch at her neck is significant. We notice that there is no cross on a similar brooch at the angel's neck, for an angel has no body to offer in sacrifice. But Mary did offer a body to her Son, mothered him, and then stood there at the cross to offer him to the Father. She wants to do the same for us. She wants to mother us who are his Body, prepare us for the Calvary that the Church must go through, and stand at the foot of our cross, encouraging us and interceding for us.

It is well then for us to recall her promise that her image would crush the serpent. This promise brings to mind the words of Genesis 3:15: "I will put enmity between you and the woman and between your offspring and hers; he will strike your head...." These words are found in the first reading of the Mass of the feast of the Immaculate Conception, and they are used by the Church to teach us that the tremendous mystery of the Immaculate Conception of the mother of Jesus is the very beginning of the downfall of Satan. Here is the one human creature over whom Satan never had dominion. We find significance too in the timing of our Lady's apparitions to Juan Diego. All of these occurred within the octave of the feast of the Immaculate Conception. This has special meaning for us Catholics of the United States; Mary is our patroness under this title. The promise of Our Lady of Guadalupe referring to her Immaculate Conception points out that from the very first moment of her existence she was filled with the Holy Spirit. Because of this it was Mary who, after the Ascension of Jesus, taught the apostles by her example and encouragement how to implore the Holy Spirit. And just as she was present in the Cenacle with the infant Church to draw down the Holy Spirit at Pentecost, so she is present with us in her image of Guadalupe as the "woman clothed with the sun, with the moon under her feet" ready to draw down once again the Holy Spirit "as in a new Pentecost."

## NOTES

1. General Sources on Fatima:
   **The Secret of Fatima,** J. M. Alonso, The Ravengate Press, Cambridge, MA 02138, 1979;
   **The Sun Danced at Fatima,** 1952, and **Exciting Fatima News,** 1979, Joseph A. Pelletier, A.A., Assumption Publications, 500 Salisbury St., Worcester, MA 01609;
   **Our Lady of Fatima,** William T. Walsh, 1954, Image Books, Doubleday and Co., Garden City, NY. (Available from AMI Press, Washington, NJ 07882.);
   **Fatima, The Great Sign,** Francis Johnston, 1979, AMI Press, Washington, NJ 07882.
2. General sources on Guadalupe:
   **A Handbook on Guadalupe,** 1974, Franciscan Marytown Press, Kenosha, WI 53142. (Now at Libertyville, IL 60048.);
   **Our Lady of Guadalupe,** George Lee, C.S.Sp., 1964, Catholic Book Publishing Co., New York, NY;
   **A Woman Clothed With the Sun,** Ethel Cook Eliot, 1961, Image Books, Doubleday and Co., Garden City, NY.

**Chapter X**

# Consecration to Mary

Consecration to Mary is key to allowing Mary to prepare us, the Bride of Christ, for the coming of the Lord Jesus. Consecration to Mary is key to achieving unity between Bride and Spirit, enabling us to call out together, "Come, Lord Jesus!" Consecration to Mary allows her to bring us toward the unity with the Spirit that she herself is now enjoying.

## Consecration to Mary and Baptism in the Holy Spirit

Our Catholic Church teaches that with the sacrament of Baptism I enter into a whole new set of relationships: that, first of all, Jesus becomes Lord of my life; that the Holy Spirit that filled him from the first moment of his conception enters my life as well; that his Father becomes my Father; that his mother becomes my mother; and that his brothers and sisters become my brothers and sisters in the Lord. The purpose of baptism in the Spirit and of Life in the Spirit Seminars or retreats, which prepared most of us who have received the baptism in the Spirit, is a deep surrender to the Spirit which allows these relationships entered into at the time of sacramental Baptism to become living realities for us.

Baptism in the Spirit has enabled countless numbers of Catholics to experience in a deep way the Lord-ship of Jesus, the guidance and power of his Spirit, and the love of his Father. It has also enabled us to come into a new relationship with brothers and sisters in the Lord Jesus, but what of the relationship between the mother of Jesus and us? Has the baptism in the Spirit conferred a new, deep experience of Mary as my mother? Some Catholics could answer in the affirmative, but all too many Catholics would have to say, "no." The question arises, "Why this discrep-ancy?" If sacramental Baptism confers all the relationships mentioned above, why does not baptism in the Spirit affect our relationship with Mary just as it affects the other relationships mentioned above? The answer to this question, we believe, lies in two basic factors: expectant faith and the historic origin of the baptism in the Spirit as experienced in the Catholic charismatic renewal.

As a general rule we receive according to the expectant faith with which we ask of God. It is true that there are exceptions to this rule. God is always free to act in unexpected ways, conferring gifts that come as a complete surprise; and at times he does so. But both Scripture and personal experience attest to his favoring us according to the faith and trust with which we ask him. Witness how often Jesus raised the level of expectant faith in a petitioner before granting his request. God's response is also conditioned by the nature of the thing requested. As a loving Father he would not answer a request for something that would prove harmful to his child. In the case of baptism in the Spirit, however, we know that what we request, namely, a coming alive of the relationships conferred in sacramental Baptism, is pleasing to him, one that he is eager to grant, because these relationships form the very foundation of our faith life.

With this in mind let us take a look at the expectant faith with which most of us in the Catholic charismatic renewal approached the baptism in the Spirit. In doing so we find that our expectancy was conditioned by the preparation we received before this event. This preparation, in turn, was deeply influenced by the historical origin of the baptism in the Spirit as we have known it. And because this origin is so recent—in the late 1960's —its influence is still strongly felt in the Catholic charismatic renewal. Catholics not only at the Duquesne weekend event but on many other occasions in places throughout the United States and abroad were prepared for and prayed over for the baptism in the Spirit by generous Pentecostals of both traditional Pentecostal denominations and mainline Protestant denominations. The expectant faith of these Pentecostals was the result of the new relationship with Jesus, his Spirit, his Father and his brothers and sisters that the baptism in the Spirit had conferred on them. When they prepared Catholics seeking the baptism of the Spirit, they shared from their own experience. When they prayed over Catholics to receive the baptism in the Spirit, they prayed for the reception of the same favors they had received. And because the gift of Mary as mother was outside their own belief and experience, a new and deeper relationship with Mary was not asked for and frequently not received. As Catholics, in turn, prepared and prayed over fellow Catholics for the baptism in the Spirit, most of them did so in a similar way. As a result, among all the relationships conferred on Catholics in sacramental Baptism the relationship with Mary was very often the one least affected by the baptism in the Spirit.

How does the consecration to Mary, recommended so warmly by our Holy Father, relate to the baptism in the Spirit we have received? It is simply the explicit turning of our lives over to Mary as mother in imitation of Jesus just as in the baptism of the Spirit we turned our lives over to Jesus himself as Lord. It is inviting her to be our mother just as we invited him to be our Lord. Where in the baptism of the Spirit we asked the Holy Spirit to form us anew into Christ, in our consecration to Mary we ask her in an explicit way to form us into Christ in union with her Spouse, the Holy Spirit. We do so because we believe that this is God's will for us, that this is what the Holy Spirit is saying to his Church at this time. He has said it through Mary herself at Fatima, when in her last apparition she extended to all her children the brown scapular to be worn as a symbol of their ongoing consecration to her, [1] and he has said it often through Pope John Paul II.

In a practical way how can consecration to Mary best be integrated into the experience of the baptism in the Spirit? We are familiar with many priests who were baptized in the Spirit after a preparation that consisted of participation in charismatic prayer meetings plus Life In The Spirit Seminars together with a daily meditative reading of the book, *Finding New Life In The Spirit*, and who later when hearing of the consecration to Mary prepared for this by participating in Cenacles of the Marian Movement of Priests and by meditative reading of the book, *Our Lady Speaks To Her Beloved Priests*, which fully supplies the specifically Catholic elements lacking in the seminars. We have also seen a priest prepare simultaneously for both these events, using the methods just described, and then at the end of a Mass experience both the baptism in the Spirit and consecration to Mary, using the formula of the Marian Movement of Priests. And we know of laity who have prepared in a somewhat similar way in order to experience both of these at the same time. There must be many ways in which these two gifts of God can be prepared for and received. The important thing is that both be recognized as essential to the full experience of our baptismal heritage and sought after with all our hearts.

It would be helpful at this point to compare baptism in the Spirit to consecration to Mary. We have already mentioned that both involve a surrender—in one to Jesus, in the other to Mary. We have also mentioned that both confer a change of relationship—in one, a new, deepened relationship with Jesus, in the other a new, deepened relationship with Mary. Both must be experienced in order to be understood, for both involve an experience of the heart that illumines the mind. In addition, a specific type of prayer characterizes those who have had each of these experiences—for one, the prayer of tongues (1 Cor. 14:2), for the other, the rosary. A beautiful effect of our consecration to Mary is that with the deepening of our relationship with her there is likewise a deepening in our praying of her rosary so that it can become contemplative prayer, prayer in the Spirit very similar to the prayer of tongues. In fact it can happen that some who pray the rosary at this depth find that they shift unconsciously into the prayer of tongues. Finally, both these experiences are open to an ever deeper surrender. Our Heavenly Father wants us to grow continually in the relationships he gave us at our sacramental Baptism. It is by surrendering ever more deeply to the Holy Spirit that we allow him to deepen these relationships. It is here that our consecration to Mary is a tremendous help, for by it we enable her to teach us the same progressive surrender to the Spirit that she experienced in her own life: Mary, the humble Virgin, was filled by the Holy Spirit even from the time of her own conception in the womb of St. Anne her mother.[2] Mary experienced an even greater fullness of the Holy Spirt as she said her "yes" to the angel Gabriel and was overshadowed by the Spirit and conceived Jesus (Luke 1:35). This experience deepened again at Calvary when she joined her "yes" with that of Jesus on the Cross (John 19:25-26). On the day of Pentecost, when Mary is especially mentioned as present, *"all* were filled with the Holy Spirit" (Acts 2:4, emphasis added.)

## Consecration is a Total Giving

Consecration is a total giving of ourselves. By consecrating ourselves to Mary we appropriate with all our hearts a relationship between ourselves and Mary that has already been established by God. Stefan Cardinal Wyszynski of Warsaw pointed this out in an address given to his priests (March 1, 1961) in preparation for the consecration of the whole Polish nation, people, priests and bishops, to Mary. He said that God repeatedly has given all to the Woman, Mary: at the Annunciation when he gave her his Son and at Calvary when Jesus from the Cross gave her every disciple whom he loves. It could be added that God gave his Holy Spirit to Mary at her conception. Cardinal Wyszynski, in language reminiscent of St. Paul's begging us by the mercy of God to offer our bodies as a living sacrifice (Rom. 12:1), begs his priests to give their all into the hands of Mary even as the Lord himself did: "We must give all to Mary; in her is our one salvation in these difficult times....I ask you, give all to our Mother Mary ....We can and must give all to the Mother of God....We are on our way to Jerusalem, to drink the cup that Jesus drank....The cup you will drink, I assure you!....But we are not alone. With us our Mother is asking and our Queen is praying."

This awareness of the richness of God's plan in

Mary was a central theme in Cardinal Wyszynski's life that deeply influenced his protege, Cardinal Wojtyla, now Pope John Paul II. At his episcopal ordination Karol Wojtyla took as his motto "Totus Tuus" ("[I Am] All Yours"), referring to Mary. He has continued to live out this consecration and asks it of all priests, people and nations.

Consecration to Mary is also spoken of as an *entrusting* of our lives to Mary. The word "to entrust" is used in a very strong and full way by Pope John Paul II. The word "to entrust" (*zawierzac* in Polish) was also used by Cardinal Wyszynski in consecrating Poland to Mary. It is a word that could well translate the motto of Pope John Paul II, "Totus Tuus", I am totally given, totally entrusted to you Mary, I am all yours. In his *Letter To All Priests*[3] our Holy Father *entrusts* all priests to Mary the Mother of Christ and asks each priest to entrust himself in a solemn yet simple way according to his own heart. Pope John Paul II understands the need and meaning of living in union with Mary and entrusting our all to her. He has lived out this consecration to Mary since the day of his ordination. As Karol Cardinal Wojtyla he said that "the *need of entrusting oneself to Mary*...flows directly from the integral logic of the faith, from rediscovery of the whole divine economy and from understanding of its mysteries." He went on to explain that, "The Father in heaven demonstrated the greatest trust in mankind by giving mankind his Son (cf John 3:16). The human creature to whom he first entrusted him was Mary, the woman of the *proto-evangelium* (cf Gen. 3:15), then Mary of Nazareth and Bethlehem, and until the end of time she will remain the one to whom God *entrusts the whole of his mystery of salvation.*"[4]

By entrusting our lives to Mary, we imitate God himself!

70

And further, we fulfill the command of the Lord to us on the Cross, "There is your mother" as we take her as our own (Jn. 19:27). This is the scriptural foundation for consecration to Mary, And we allow Mary to fulfill the command Jesus gave to her, that is, to form us as sons (Jn. 19:26). By entrusting our lives to her we unite our "yes" with her "yes" of Nazareth and of Calvary. By entrusting our lives to her we draw down the Spirit and make possible the new Pentecost.

## NOTES

1. Pope Pius XII said in a letter written in 1950 commemorating the seventh centenary of Our Lady's giving of the scapular to St. Simon Stock: "Take this scapular, which Our Lady has given as a sign of consecration to her Immaculate Heart."
2. **Lumen Gentium,** #56, Second Vatican Council.
3. Holy Thursday, 1979, N.C.C.B., 1312 Massachusetts Ave., N.W., Washington, D.C. 20005.
4. **Signs of Contradiction,** Lenten Retreat given to Pope Paul VI, 1976, The Seabury Press, New York, NY 10017; emphasis added.

# Part Three

# Come, Lord Jesus!

"Our era is the era of the Immaculata, or as others put it, the era of the Holy Spirit."[1] We believe these words, spoken by Blessed Maximilian Kolbe in 1936, to be truly prophetic. At first sight these may seem strange words with which to introduce a section dealing with the reign of Jesus. Yet, the era of the Immaculata, or of the Holy Spirit, is essential in God's plan for ushering in the era of Jesus' reign.

In Chapter VIII, we indicated the sources (particularly the writings of Blessed Maximilian Kolbe) which show that Mary is inseparable from the Holy Spirit. It follows, then, that the era of the Immaculata is in a very true sense the era of the Holy Spirit.

Not only that, but both Mary and the Spirit point to Jesus. As we mentioned at the end of Chapter VIII, the Spirit within us delights in pointing out that "Jesus is Lord." It is true that he also delights in pointing out that "Mary is mother", but this he does in order that she, in turn, can point to Jesus as Lord. She did this at the beginning of his public ministry when at Cana she told the servants, "Do whatever he tells you" (John 2:5). These words evoked Jesus' first miracle, launching him into his public life. These words also sum up the message of Our Lady in her apparitions of the past century and a half. Her urgent plea to us for sacrifice and prayers simply echoes the same plea of her Son that we take up our cross daily (Luke 9:23) and pray always (Luke 18:1). The Angel of Fatima summed up her message in these words: "Pray! Pray a great deal!...Offer up prayers and sacrifices to the Most High....Make everything you do a sacrifice, and offer it as an act of reparation for the sins by which he is offended and in supplication for the conversion of sinners....Above all, accept and bear with submission the sufferings sent you by Our Lord." And in his next apparition he revealed how to make these sacrifices and prayers effective: by offering them in union with the Eucharistic Sacrifice.

Now, in *Our Lady Speaks to Her Beloved Priests,* Mary reveals that her pleas for sacrifice and prayer are about to be fully answered. She reveals that the "hour" for the Bride has finally arrived, the corporate sacrifice of Calvary preparing for the corporate prayer of the Cenacle. She reveals that her Son has appointed her to guide us through our Calvary and Cenacle. And she reveals that the essential step we must take in order to receive her guidance is to consecrate ourselves to her.

In Part III, we treat of the united cry of Spirit and Bride, a cry raised from both Cross and Cenacle, imploring Jesus to come quickly and establish his reign in our hearts.

## NOTES

1. H. M. Manteau-Bonamy, **Immaculate Conception and the Holy Spirit: The Marian Teachings of Father Kolbe,** 1977, Prow Books, Kenosha, WI 53142, p. 63.

# Chapter XI

# The Anguished Cry of the Bride

We believe that Mary's specific role in the present time is to prepare the Church for Calvary. The Church is entering into a time of corporate Calvary, a time of anguish and travail. The purpose of our dealing with this tribulation within the Church is that we might understand that this is God's work of preparation and of purification and not be scandalized and depressed at the confusion, insubordination, dissent and even persecution within the Church itself. We believe that signs of tribulation will worsen before they get better and we need to understand that the mystery of God's plan of death and resurrection is at work.

There are many facets to the mystery of suffering and the Cross. In no way do these reflections exhaust them. Suffering purifies and disciplines (Heb. 5:8-9) for further growth (Heb. 12:1-13), fostering endurance (Rom. 5:3-4) and maturity (James 1:4), proves our love (John 13:34-35) and so prepares us for glory (Rom. 8:18). It is also a healing experience as we learn to discern the origins of sufferings and decide whether to reject them or embrace them. If the suffering is from our own sin, we repent and reject the sin, and healing follows. If it is God's paschal mystery at work for the sake of the Gospel, we embrace it and rejoice at his salvation at work. Suffering is redemptive when embraced as the Cross of Jesus Christ because it brings salvation not only to ourselves but also to others. The ultimate origin of suffering is sin, and one antidote for sin is redemptive suffering.

### Suffering is not...

Suffering is not meaningless, but rather when embraced as the Cross of Christ, it becomes "the power of God and the wisdom of God" (1 Cor. 1:24). It is not simply the punishment of a wrathful God, but it is the mercy of God at work which the humble, poor and repentant experience as loving kindness, but which the proud and unrepentant sinners experience as God's wrath disciplining them. It is not useless, but rather is tremendously precious because it brings salvation to souls by applying the power of the Cross to their need. We do not seek pain or inflict it on ourselves for its own sake, but rather endure the Cross for the sake of the life and joy that lie ahead (cf Heb. 12:2). Nor is redemptive suffering a rejection of healing; rather, it is a way of bringing total healing, that is, salvation to ourselves and to others. One effect of healing is that it removes the obstacles within us that prevent us from recognizing the Cross and embracing it with joy.

### The Wisdom of the Cross

To grasp the folly of the Cross as the power of God and the wisdom of God takes a wisdom that is pure gift. Without this wisdom all suffering, pain and the Cross of Christ are utter foolishness and a stumbling block. If we don't have this wisdom, we need to acquire it at any price! Fortunately, St. James tells us it is available for the *asking*, as long as we ask with faith and patient perseverance: "My brothers, count it pure joy when you are involved in every sort of trial. Realize that when your faith is tested it makes for endurance. Let endurance come to its perfection so that you may mature in everything. If any of you is without wisdom, let him ask for it from God who gives generously and ungrudgingly to all, and it will be given him. Yet he must ask in faith, never doubting..." (James 1:2-6).

Suffering is the wisdom and power of God when it is the Cross of Christ. Precisely, the Cross is the wisdom and power of God because it is the Cross that is the answer to sin, to Satan and to death itself. Only the suffering of Christ crucified, Head and Body, brings salvation from sin and its consequences, namely, the domination of Satan and death. It is by dying that we are born to eternal life. Only by losing our life can we gain life (Matthew 16:25). This is the wisdom of God.

## The Role of the Sorrowful Mother

By Mary's "yes" on Calvary to God's plan of total sacrificial love, the Church was conceived and Mary became its mother. She shared in this total act of sacrificial love by her "yes". Her heart too was pierced, as she offered her Son's sufferings. At that moment she was the public person representing the whole Church. It was then and there at the Cross that she was explicitly commissioned by Jesus to prepare the Bride to follow in the pattern of the Bridegroom. She was commissioned to prepare the Bride by purifying our "yes" to be like hers, so that the whole Christ, Head and Body, could offer a total sacrifice of love to the Father. Her "yes" as the public person is now to be offered by the Church as a corporate person.

Mary now seeks our consecration to her so that she might prepare us and bring us to the docile "yes" of Jesus on the Cross. She needs our consecration and not

just a vague devotion and piety. Rather, she needs our
devotion and piety in the root meaning of the words,
i.e., "devotion" as the giving of our vows
(consecration) and "piety" as the response of loving
sons.

To grasp this vision of God's plan to prepare his
Bride for the "new age", we need a new wisdom. This
new wisdom is especially available to those who have
consecrated themselves to Mary, the Seat of Wisdom.
Many of these will soon begin to experience the Cross
in their daily lives. They may well begin to wonder,
"What has happened to me?" A lesson can be learned
from an experience common to those who have been
baptized in the Holy Spirit. The latter soon find
themselves in combat with the evil spirit just as Jesus,
as soon as he was baptized in the Holy Spirit in the
Jordan, was led into the desert to do combat with Satan
(Mark 1: 10-13). In a somewhat similar way, those who
consecrate themselves to Mary in this time of travail
may soon experience the Cross. In both the baptism in
the Holy Spirit and in consecration to Mary the Holy
Spirit is at work encountering sin and Satan. Rejoice,
because the power of God is at work!

## Offering Our Suffering Eucharistically

The old phrase "offer it up" seems to have disap-
peared from our modern vocabulary. With the loss of
the practice of "offering it up" we have lost in practice
the experience of participating in the Eucharist as
sacrifice. The sacrificial element of the Eucharist is an
essential one: it is the sacrifice of Jesus, our Head, and
of the Church, his Body. The Second Vatican Council
made this clear in the *Constitution on the Sacred
Liturgy:* "At the Last Supper, on the night when he
was betrayed, our Savior instituted the Sacrifice of

His Body and Blood. He did this in order to perpetuate the sacrifice of the Cross through the centuries until He should come again, and so to entrust to His Beloved Spouse, the Church, a memorial of His death and resurrection."[1]

To enter into the Eucharistic Sacrifice deeply is to enter into deeper intercession. It is to drink the cup that Jesus drank and be baptized in the same bath of pain. When we "offer it up", Jesus speaks to us as he spoke to James and John: "From the cup I drink you shall drink; the bath (of pain) I am immersed in you shall share" (Mark 10:39).

Suffering is so precious to God that it seems he allows it to continue until the last moment, as he did with his own Son. If suffering is so precious, we should not waste any of it, not even the most insignificant or confused pain, but "offer it up".

It is precisely here that the role of Mary, the Mother of Sorrows, is most effective. She has been commissioned by Jesus on the Cross (John 19:26) to prepare us for this baptism of suffering as she did Jesus. She wants to bring us to the docility of Jesus on the Cross, a docility of total trust and obedience, offering this as a sacrifice to the Father. By entrusting to her all that we are, by our consecration to her Sorrowful and Immaculate Heart, we enable her to transform our weaknesses and our burdened hearts and thus prepare us for the Eucharistic Sacrifice. She then will "offer us up" as a pleasing sacrifice to the Father, uniting us with the Sacrifice of Jesus for the salvation of the world.

How much more fully does all this apply to the priest who by his ordination is called to "offer up" himself and the people. He is called to be victim and intercessor in union with Christ Jesus, the innocent Lamb who laid down his life to take away the sins of the world.

78

In victim-intercession we face one of the great mysteries of our faith. It can confuse the greatest minds, yet it is so simple that even a child can practice it! At Our Lady's request the three little children of Fatima entered into this atonement for sinners wholeheartedly, "offering up" their sacrifices and suffering in union with the Eucharistic Sacrifice. Here is a great mystery revealed to the little ones that the learned and clever cannot see (Luke 10:21). Here is a great mystery that needs to be rediscovered and experienced by the whole Church.

### The Anguished Cry of the Bride from the Cross

Today, in this time of travail, the broken Body of Christ is on the Cross. The great anguished cry for mercy needs to rise up to heaven: "Father, in your mercy send your Son, Jesus. Jesus, in your mercy come in glory!" This is *the* great cry of anguish of the Bride. The Church is living out the Eucharist. As Jesus, our Head, cried from the Cross, "Father, forgive them, for they do not know what they are doing." (Luke 23:34), so too his broken Body needs to call out, "Father, have mercy on us and the whole world! Look at the broken Body of your Son and have mercy!"

At the Cross the Bride is prepared for the work of the Cenacle.

### NOTES

1. **Sacrosanctum Concilium, #47.**

**Chapter XII**

# United
# Intercession
# for the
# New Pentecost

Pope John XXIII's prayer for a new Pentecost calls for united intercession by the Church: "...praying perseveringly and insistently with one heart and mind together with Mary, the Mother of Jesus, and guided by blessed Peter...." This prayer echoes the description of the apostles and Mary and the women praying for the first Pentecost (Acts 1:14).

In the first Pentecost there were certain prerequisites for the sovereign act of God: *wait* for the Power from on high, *intercede together with Mary and Peter* (cf Luke 24:49; Acts 1:4-8, 14). If we are to do something in preparation for the new Pentecost, then we have a model in what was done to prepare for the first: 1) wait, 2) intercede, 3) together, 4) in union with Mary and 5) Peter. The new Pentecost, too, will be a sovereign act of God, and he has set his own conditions for its fulfillment.

## 1] Wait...

Wait for the power from on high (Luke 24:49). Wait for the soversign act of God! It is God's power, his plan and his priorities that are involved here. It is his timing of events that will accomplish this act through the power of his Holy Spirit. Our anxiety and our feverish activity will not hasten the day of the Lord, but our patience and enduring trust will. During the time of waiting the Lord prepares and purifies us for his plan to be accomplished through us. During this time we are to listen to the Lord, to learn his plan and be prepared to act upon it.

## 2] Intercede...

During this time we are to intercede for God's mercy. We are to devote ourselves to constant prayer, asking forgiveness for our own lack of unity, asking for his kingdom to come among us, asking for a sovereign act of God to unite a divided Christianity, asking for the new Pentecost.

This prayer is an intense cry of intercession calling for a new Pentecost, a renewed Church, the Kingdom of glory. This cry is addressed to the Holy Spirit to act in a new and wonderful way in this our age.

Pope Paul VI prayed in this intense way when, reflecting on the turmoil and travail of the Church, he exhorted us to implore the Holy Spirit and listen to him.[1] He hoped and prayed for a new Pentecost:

"One must also recognize a prophetic intuition on the part of our predecessor John XXIII, who envisaged a kind of new Pentecost as a fruit of the Council. We too have wished to place ourself in the same perspective and in the same attitude of expectation. Not that Pentecost has ever ceased to be an actuality during the whole history of the Church, but so great are the needs and the perils of the present age, so vast the horizon of mankind drawn toward world coexistence and powerless to achieve it, that *there is no salvation for it except in a new outpouring of the gift of God.* Let him then come, the Creating Spirit, to renew the face of the earth!"[2]

In a similar and even more intense way Pope John Paul II exhorted us in his first encyclical to "appeal to the Spirit as the answer to all the materialisms."[3] In concluding his encyclical he shared his feeling of need for intense intercession: "We feel not only the need but even a categorical imperative for great, intense and growing prayer by all the Church."[4] He immediately went on to state the need of prayer in this time of difficulties. "Only prayer can prevent all these succeeding tasks and difficulties from becoming a source of crises and make them instead the occasion and, as it were, the foundation for even more mature achievements on the People of God's march towards the Promised Land."[5]

The Church prays most intensely and effectively when it is united with one heart and mind in the Eucharist. In the Eucharist, the Church invokes the Holy Spirit upon the gifts and upon itself and unites with the whole heavenly court to intercede for the Church and world. For this reason we have devoted the following chapter to the Eucharist as intercession.

## 3] Together...

The unity Jesus prayed for (cf John 17) must begin with ourselves. Our own hearts cannot be divided. This calls for a continuous repentance. It also calls for a sincere seeking for the ways to unity with each other.

Jesus taught us the power of united prayer: "Again I tell you, if two of you join your voices on earth to pray for anything whatever, it shall be granted you by my Father in heaven" (Matthew 18:19). Our experience has shown us that the hardest part of this teaching is to

82

be united in one voice, that is, agreed in heart and mind on any given topic. This kind of unity in the Lord demands listening, understanding, submission, forgiveness and commitment to the agreed upon truth—these are the very basic ingredients of Christian community. It is the united Christian community, united in heart and mind, joining together its voice in common intercession, that is the fundamental unit of the praying Church.

## 4] In Union with Mary...

Mary's role is precisely to prepare the Bride of Christ, the Church, to be one with the Spirit as she herself is, and so intercede in a united way for the coming of the Lord Jesus. By consecration to Mary we allow her to prepare us as the spotless Bride of Christ. We must realize, however, that her way of preparing the Bride for the work of the Cenacle is by way of the Cross. She takes literally our consecration to her as she teaches us the docility of Jesus himself. Mary prepares the Bride to be "in Christ a kind of sacrament of intimate union with God, and of the unity of all mankind",[6] in order to intercede for the new Pentecost.

## 5] and Peter

Unity with Peter in the person of his successor, the reigning Pope, is expressed in our loyalty and reverence as we listen to him, obey him, support him in our teachings, pray for him and with him, and love him. He is the visible expression of unity in the Church and the visible sign of Christ's presence as head of his Church. Our unity with Peter is extended to all bishops in union with him and in a particular way to our local ordinary.

The most effective steps we can take toward the new Pentecost are those taken in union with Mary, the Mother of the Church, and in union with the successor of Peter and the Apostles, because God has made this twofold union an essential condition for his sovereign act.

## NOTES

1. **Ecclesiam Suam,** #26.
2. **Gaudete in Domino,** VII, emphasis added.
3. See **Redemptor Hominis,** #18.
4. ibid, #22.
5. ibid, #22.
6. **Lumen Gentium**, #1, Second Vatican Council.

# Chapter XIII

# The Eucharist, Summit of United Intercession

The Eucharist as an expression of united intercession presents a problem. It was instituted as a sign of unity; yet, right from the beginning and continuing down to the present, it has all too often revealed *disunity* among the followers of Christ. The Last Supper was the occasion for bickering among the apostles as to who was the greatest among them. Peter boasted about his loyalty, Judas left to betray Jesus, and the rest fled soon after the Sacred Meal. In the early Church at Corinth St. Paul had to deal with disorder and party spirits in the celebration of the Eucharist. And this picture has continued right down to our day with a litany of problems centered around the Eucharist: divisions between Churches over differences of interpretation, party loyalties, and denominationalism that have fractured the Body of Christ so that a common Eucharist cannot be celebrated.

A significant moment that illustrated the lack of unity needed for a common Eucharist was the Conference on Charismatic Renewal in the Christian Churches held at Kansas City, July 20 to 24, 1977. Over 50,000 Christians from the various traditions in the charismatic renewal came together for the first time. It was a dramatic demonstration of the *desire* for unity in a divided Church. Kevin Ranaghan, the chairman of the

Conference, told the opening session, "I believe that God has spoken this conference as a living prophecy in the Church and to the world, that he has decided to have one people, one bride." But the conference was also a dramatic demonstration of disunity because the Eucharist could not be celebrated together. Ten different denominations held mini-conferences within the larger conference, and each celebrated its own liturgy of the breaking of the bread, dramatizing the fact of the broken Body of Christ.

### Yielding to Unity...Together with Mary

There are conditions that need to be fulfilled before the Eucharist can be celebrated as "the center and culmination of the whole life of the Christian community."[1] The basic conditions can be stated in the words of the prayer of Pope John XXIII: we need to intercede "with one heart and mind together with Mary, the Mother of Jesus, and guided by blessed Peter."

It seems that the Eucharist is the focal point of the spiritual battle for unity. Here the forces of Satan seem to work the hardest to prevent the celebration of a united Eucharist. For our Eucharist to be united and so effective, we need to yield to the Spirit, even as the gifts of bread and wine might be said to yield to the Holy Spirit and so become the Body and Blood of our Lord Jesus Christ. Since they offer no resistance to the Spirit, they become what they signify. If we offer no resistance to the Spirit we too become the Body of Christ.

Our model and mother of this yielding to the Holy Spirit is our mother Mary. As *model* she shows us what it means to yield, to live in a continual "yes" to the Father. As *mother* she transforms our weak "yes" to her own by her powerful intercession. Our "yes" of entrusting our lives to her, enables her to say of us as she can truly say of Jesus, "This is my body; this is my blood."

It is in this yielding by our total consecration that we live out the "Totus Tuus" of self-sacrifice. It is in sacrifice that we most effectively repent of self-concern and the sin of disunity and give ourselves for the sake of the kingdom. It is in union with the sacrifice of Jesus that our intercession becomes united with his and so effective.

It is precisely in yielding that we enter into the cooperative work of the Holy Spirit and Mary, bringing forth the Body of Jesus. We, the Body of Christ, are born even as the Head, Jesus, of the Virgin Mary by the power of the Holy Spirit. When we yield to the Spirit, we also yield to Mary; and when we yield to Mary, we also yield to the Spirit.

### United Intercession

Like no other action of the Church, the celebration of the Eucharist must be *the* act of intercession. It is in this action above all that the Church must be united with Christ the High Priest at the right hand of the Father interceding for us. And by the same token this celebration demands unity within the Church. If we are not in unity, we are told by Jesus to leave our gift at the altar and be reconciled with our brother (cf Matthew 5:23-24). It is especially at the Eucharist that the Spirit and the Bride are to be united in their cry, "Come, Lord Jesus!"

Without this unity we eat and drink the Body and Blood of the Lord to our own judgment and show contempt for the Church of God. Such celebration of the Eucharist brings about sickness, weakness and deaths

88

in the community (cf 1 Cor. 11:17-34). On the other hand we express our unity when we recognize with faith and obedience the assembly with its pastors as the Body of the Lord and examine ourselves before eating of this bread and drinking of this cup. It is in this united action that we remember the Lord Jesus. Every time, then, that we are united in faith and obedience while eating this bread and drinking this cup we "proclaim the death of the Lord until he comes" (1 Cor. 11:26).

## The United Cry of "Come, Lord Jesus!"

The united proclamation of the Church in the Eucharist is a proclamation of the Lord's death until he comes. It is in this united cry of "Come!" that the Church expresses the summit of intercession. It is the united cry of the Spirit and the Bride proclaiming the death of the Lord *until* he comes in glory. The word "until" according to J. Jeremias[2] expresses not only time but also purpose, and thus could also be translated "in order that." The united Eucharistic intercession of the Spirit and the Bride, then, effect the coming of the Lord Jesus! And further, each time the united Eucharist is celebrated, it is a reminder to the Father that the work of Jesus is not yet complete...He is yet to come in glory! The words of the prophet Isaiah apply here: "Upon your walls, O Jerusalem, I have stationed watchmen; never by day or by night, shall they be silent. O you who are to remind the Lord, take no rest and give no rest to him until he re-establishes Jerusalem, and makes it the pride of the earth." (Isaiah 62:6-7. And again: "Then you shall call, and the Lord will answer, you shall cry for help, and he will say, "Here I am!" (Isaiah 58:9).

## NOTES

1. **Christus Dominus**, #30, Second Vatican Council.
2. **The Eucharistic Words of Jesus**, J. Jeremias, SCM Press, London, 1966, p. 253.

# Chapter XIV

# Increasing the Reign of the Divine Savior

God's plan to increase the reign of the Divine Savior is different from man's plan. One of the prophecies given at St. Peter's Basilica during the closing Eucharist on the day after Pentecost, May 19, 1975, spoke of a "new age" and a new combat for which we will need new wisdom, new power, and new understanding of his plan:

"I speak to you of the dawn of a new age for my church. I speak to you of a day that has not been seen before....Prepare yourselves for the action that I begin now, because things that you see around you will change; the combat that you must enter now is different; it is new. You need wisdom from me that you do not yet have. You need the power of my Holy Spirit in a way that you have not possessed it; you need an understanding of my will and of the ways that I work that you do not yet have. Open your eyes, open your hearts to prepare yourselves for me and for the day that I have now begun. My church will be different; my people will be different; difficulties and trials will come upon you. The comfort that you know now will be far from you, but the comfort that you will have is the comfort of my Holy Spirit. They will send for you, to take your life, but I will support you. Come to me. Band yourselves together around me. Prepare, for I proclaim a new day, a day of victory and of triumph for your God. Behold, it is begun."[1]

## By a Sovereign Act of God

The "dawning of a new age" for the Church involves a sovereign act of God, that is, God acting in his own way to bring it about. It means that our own wisdom, power and understanding are not only inadequate but rather, far worse, they are counter-productive and so hinder the increase of the reign of God. Our preparation for the new age is to open our eyes and hearts and turn to the Lord to receive his wisdom, power and understanding.

In his prayer Pope John XXIII asks that the Church "may increase the reign of the Divine Savior" through a sovereign act of God, a new Pentecost. The English word "increase" does not convey all the richness of the Latin word "amplificet" which does mean *to increase* but also carries with it the meaning of bringing to fulfillment. Pope John XXIII, then, asks the Divine Spirit to renew his wonders in this our age and usher in the resplendent reign of Jesus as Lord. He asks that the Church may be instrumental in bringing about the reign of the Divine Savior by hastening the Day of the Lord (2 Peter 3:12).

In order to be a truly effective instrument of the Lord as he prepares us for his sovereign act, the Church must make full use of the following:

* *Prophecy:* The Lord has spoken in our time through papal exhortations, revelations authenticated by the Church, Marian messages and charismatic prophecies concerning the nature of the kingdom.

* *Repentance and Conversion:* It is the time to

call all mankind to repentance and conversion beginning with ourselves.

* *Consecration to Mary:* This is God's condition for bringing about the sovereign act of God, ushering in his reign.
* *Travail:* The present time of ever-worsening tribulation of the Church and world is God's Paschal Mystery at work, purifying us by the Cross, preparing us for his reign.
* *Spiritual Warfare:* The present travail is spiritual warfare. "Our battle is not against human forces but against the principalities and powers, the rulers of this world of darkness" (Ephesians 6:12).
* *Suffering as Victim-Intercessors:* The time calls for applying the full power of the Cross which means suffering as victims with Christ, united with him in his work of redemption and salvation of the world.
* *Imploring the Spirit:* It is time to implore God to send his Holy Spirit to bring about his kingdom, and this is the work of the Church in the Upper Room preparing for the new Pentecost.

These elements need to be part of "increasing the reign of the Divine Savior;" otherwise we are increasing our own reign and building our own city according to our own plan.

### By the Spirit of Truth and Love

Only the gift of God, the Holy Spirit, can bring about the reign described in the prayer of Pope John XXIII, "The reign of truth and justice, the reign of love and peace." When justice and peace are sought without seeking the equally necessary truth and love, they are sought in vain. To establish God's justice and peace, then, the only real justice and peace, we must first be filled with the Spirit of truth (John 14:17) and of love (Romans 5:5). Why? Because we are basically fighting the father of lies (John 8:44) and of murders (John 8:40-41), not simply unjust men or even unjust institutions. We are truly engaged in spiritual warfare for which the resources of unaided man are totally inadequate. Only the Holy Spirit can equip us for this kind of warfare. Significantly Pope Leo XIII, who in his encyclical *Rerum Novarum* gave the Church a beautiful charter for social justice, also provided the Church with three powerful weapons for spiritual warfare: an exorcism invoking the aid of St. Michael the archangel which the Church prayed at the end of Mass for many years, a novena to the Holy Spirit to be offered yearly before Pentecost by the entire Church, and no less than nine encyclicals urging the fervent praying of Our Lady's rosary. With this in mind let us look at the couplets which describe the reign of Christ.

### "The reign of truth *and* justice..."

It is a reign of justice based on the truth of Jesus Christ, true God and true man who lived, suffered, died and rose from the dead so that we might live with his justice. It is not a reign of justice according to man's standards, one independent of God, but a justice that is God's own righteousness, his very holiness. Without truth, that is, without Jesus Christ there is no justice. It is the Spirit of truth that will guide us to all truth (John 16:13).

### "The reign of love *and* peace..."

It is a reign of peace based on the love of Christ which is a gift of God. When Christ gives his peace, it is with his love and not as the world gives. The world gives peace that is a false peace, that depends on being fully armed with man's weapons of war. More and more Americans are realizing that the arms for which they have spent hundreds of billions of dollars are incapable of guaranteeing peace. Only God's plan, which involves consecration to Mary and the sacrifice and prayer she has asked for, can accomplish this. God's plan, when compared to our nation's elaborate defense plan, is extremely simple. Yet it was through obedience to just such a word of the Lord that Naaman washed seven times in the Jordan and was completely healed of his leprosy (2 Kings 5). The true peace of Christ comes as a gift and is the love of the Holy Spirit poured into our hearts (Romans 5:5). His love is our armor. The true peace of Christ flows out of love and not out of hatred as does the peace of the world. True peace follows upon repentance and forgiveness (John 20:22-23). Without love there is no peace. It is the Spirit of love breathed upon us by the victorious Lord Jesus that gives peace (John 20:19-23).

The Church will increase the reign of the Divine Savior by returning to the Upper Room by way of Calvary! United with Jesus on the Cross and with Mary we need to offer our brokenness for the salvation of the world. United with Mary and Peter in the Upper Room we need to implore the Spirit for a new Pentecost. *Then* filled with the power of the Holy Spirit we can go forth to the market place and proclaim the good news of salvation: repent, believe, be baptized in the name of Jesus Christ for the forgiveness of sins. Receive the gift of the Holy Spirit. Enter the community and be saved from this generation (cf Acts 2:36-47). We need to receive the Holy Spirit in power before we can be dispensers of the good news of salvation. "You can't give what you don't have." The reign of the Divine

96

Savior is a gift which we must receive and experience in order to share with others. The words of Pope Paul VI become ever more urgent: "There is no salvation for this present age except in a new outpouring of the gift of God."[2]

1. Text from **New Covenant,** July, 1975.
2. **Gaudete in Dominus,** Chapter VII, 1975.

# Chapter XV

# The Call to be Fully Bride

The invitation the Holy Spirit has been giving to our Church since the beginning of this century is the invitation to become fully Bride. This is the purpose of the new Pentecost and the resplendent reign of Jesus. Put in another way, the Spirit within us has been urging us to experience the fulness of Christianity that he has in mind for us—in other words, to experience normal Christianity.

What do we mean by normal Christianity? In a penetrating analysis of the makeup of normal Christianity, Father Francis Martin states that it is composed of five basic ingredients:

1. To know Jesus personally, experientially, and to give your whole life to him as Lord.

2. To live in conscious awareness of the power of the Holy Spirit who enables us to say, "Abba" and who, when we ask with faith, gives us the charismatic gifts, the tools of love for building the Body of Christ.

3. To live in community with others, a community having real authority and submission as well as a network of committed relationships, with the Eucharist at its heart of faith.

Before going on to the remaining two, let us pause and note that these first three ingredients are what we pointed to in Chapter I as fruits of the sovereign action of the Holy Spirit in the charismatic renewal, fruits which many Catholics have experienced during the past decade. Expressed briefly, these fruits can be termed conversion, charisma, and community. They have resulted from the act of surrender to Jesus and his Spirit made when we were baptized in the Holy Spirit. This new release of the Spirit's activity in our lives has enabled us to live out more fully the three sacraments of initiation by actually experiencing the conversion to Christ assumed in Baptism, the outpouring of the Spirit and his gifts in Confirmation and the community with brothers and sisters in Christ that is assumed in the sacrament of Holy Eucharist.

Father Martin then gives the last two ingredients:

4. To have these communities related to one another in perfect unity.

5. To show forth the normal Christian life in the fruits of service, primarily evangelization and the preaching of the word of God with power.

He goes on to say with reference to the fourth ingredient, "We have to admit that nobody lives the normal Christian life, because the Body of Christ is not one. In a sense, we are all living in a state of sin, because we are all living in a divided Church. The Body of Christ is divided, and therefore it is not according to God's will: it is not normal."[1]

We have expressed our conviction that a sovereign act of God is needed to bring about the perfect unity among Christian communities that characterizes normal Christianity. And it should be clear, in turn, that only from a perfectly united Christianity can truly effective evangelization proceed. Our Lord's words at the Last Supper make this clear: "I pray that they may be one in us, that the world may believe that you sent me" (John 17:21). Only when we Christians are one will the world be willing to believe in Christ. Every foreign missioner can attest to the scandal of a divided Christianity and the obstacle it places to evangelization.

Only a sovereign outpouring of the Holy Spirit in the new Pentecost can bring about perfect Christian unity and a time of true evangelization. And only the same outpouring of the Spirit of truth and love into the hearts of Christians living in such unity can produce the loving service that will bring true justice and peace to a needy world.

What, then, do we believe God is asking of those Catholics who have experienced the first two or three ingredients of normal Christianity and who are hungering for the rest? We believe he is asking you to experience the sacraments of initiation at an even deeper level than you experienced with the baptism in the Holy Spirit. Beyond your conversion through faith in Christ he is asking of you corporate crucifixion with Christ. Beyond your use of the charisms he is asking for your united imploring of the Spirit in the Cenacle. Beyond your individual communities he is asking for the fully-united Church of the new Pentecost where all will dine together at the table of the Lord and serve one another with love.

And how are you to answer this call? By becoming a child—a little child of Mary. By completing your surrender to Jesus and the Spirit in accepting his invitation to surrender also to Mary, for this is what consecration to Mary means. It is assuming the role of the "beloved disciple" of Jesus and letting Mary guide you to the Cross, then through the Cenacle to become fully Church.

What of those Catholics who have not yet experienced the basic ingredients of normal Christianity? Our answer is the same as for those who have. Entrust your lives to Mary. She and her Spouse, the Holy Spirit, will provide you with these ingredients to help you hasten the sovereign act that ushers in the reign of Christ. Recall how she raised eight million Aztecs from the pagan practice of human sacrifice to Christianity in less than a decade. You will experience the truth of what the angel told Mary "...nothing is impossible with God" (Luke 1:37). It is his will that all of us receive the precious gift he has given our Church in Mary, taking her into our hearts, allowing her to guide us to the new Pentecost.

NOTES

1. **"Nothing Less than Normal," New Covenant,** December, 1978.

## Epilogue

# An Act of
# Consecration to Mary

*Mary, Mother of Jesus and Mother of Mercy,*
*since Jesus from the Cross gave you to me,*
*I take you as my own.*
*And since Jesus gave me to you,*
*take me as your own.*
*Make me docile like Jesus on the Cross,*
*obedient to the Father,*
*trusting in humility and in love.*

*Mary, my Mother, in imitation of the Father,*
*who gave his Son to you,*
*I too give my all to you:*
*to you I entrust all that I am,*
*all that I have and all that I do.*
*Help me to surrender ever more fully to the Spirit.*
*Lead me deeper into the Mystery*
*of the Cross, the Cenacle and the fullness of Church.*
*As you formed the heart of Jesus by the Spirit,*
*form my heart to be the throne of Jesus*
*in his glorious coming.*

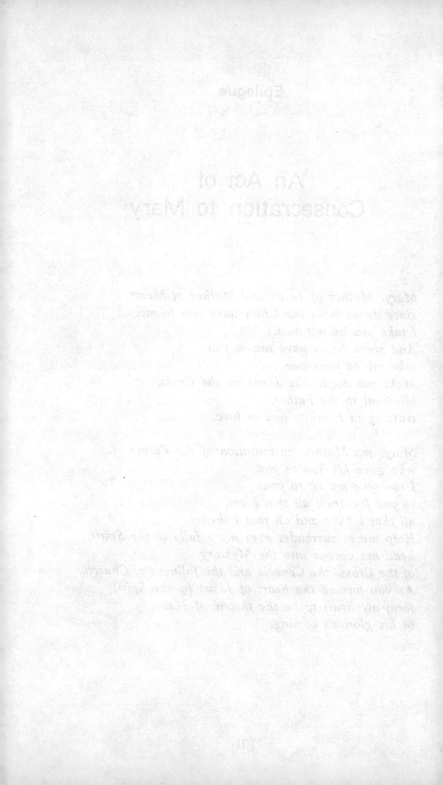

**Appendix**

# Words of Pope John Paul II at Fatima, May 13, 1982

The text of the consecration to Mary by Pope John Paul II at Fatima, May 13, 1982, is included in this second printing because it is a powerful and clear statement of the message of this book.

## Act of Consecration of the World and Russia to the Immaculate Heart

"We have recourse to your protection, holy Mother of God."

As I utter the words of this antiphon with which the Church of Christ has prayed for centuries, I find myself today in this place chosen by you, O Mother, and by you particularly loved.

I am here, united with all the Pastors of the Church in that particular bond whereby we constitute a body and a college, just as Christ desired the Apostles to be in union with Peter.

In the bond of this union, I utter the words of the present Act, in which I wish to include, once more, the hopes and anxieties of the Church in the modern world.

Forty years ago and again ten years later, your servant Pope Pius XII, having before his eyes the painful experience of the human family, entrusted and consecrated to your Immaculate Heart the whole world, and especially the peoples for which you had particular love and solicitude.

This world of individuals and nations I too have before my eyes today, as I renew the entrusting and consecration carried out by my Predecessor in the See of Peter: the world of the second millennium that is drawing to a close, the modern world, our world today!

The Church, mindful of the Lord's words: "God . . . and make disciples of all nations . . . and lo, I am with you always, to the close of the age" (Mt 28:19-20), renewed, at the Second Vatican Council, her awareness of her mission in this world.

And therefore, O Mother of individuals and peoples, you who "know all their sufferings and hopes", you who have a mother's awareness of all the struggles between good and evil, between light and darkness, which afflict the modern world, accept the cry which we, as though moved by the Holy Spirit, address directly to your Heart. Embrace, with the love of the Mother and Handmaid, this human world of ours, which we entrust and consecrate to you, for we are full of disquiet for the earthly and eternal destiny of individuals and peoples.

In a special way we entrust and consecrate to you those individuals and nations which particularly need to be entrusted and consecrated.

"We have recourse to your protection, holy Mother of God: reject not the prayers we send up to you in our necessities."

Reject them not!

Accept our humble trust — and our act of entrusting!

"For God so loved the world that he gave his only Son, that whoever believes in him should not perish but have eternal life" (Jn 3:16).

It was precisely by reason of this love that the Son of God consecrated himself for all mankind: "And for their sake I consecrate myself, that they also may be consecrated in truth" (Jn 17:19).

By reason of that consecration the disciples of all ages are called to expend themselves for the salvation of the world, and to supplement Christ's afflictions for the sake of his body, that is the Church (cf. 2 Cor. 12:15; Col. 1:24).

Before you, Mother of Christ, before your Immaculate Heart, I today, together with the whole Church, unite myself with our Redeemer in this his consecration for the world and for people, which only in his divine Heart has the power to obtain pardon and to secure reparation.

The power of this consecration lasts for all time and embraces all individuals, peoples and nations. It overcomes every evil that the spirit of darkness is able to awaken, and has in fact awakened in our times, in the heart of man and in his history.

The Church, the Mystical Body of Christ, unites herself, through the service of Peter's successor, to this consecration by our Redeemer.

Oh, how deeply we feel the need for consecration on the part of humanity and of the world — our modern world — in union with Christ himself! The redeeming work of Christ, in fact, must be shared in by the world by means of the Church.

Oh, how pained we are by all the things in the Church and in each one of us that are opposed to holiness and consecration! How pained we are that the invitation to repentance, to conversion, to prayer, has not met with the acceptance that it should have received!

How pained are we that many share so coldly in Christ's work of Redemption! That "what is lacking in Christ's afflictions" is so insufficiently completed in our flesh.

And so, blessed be all those souls that obey the call of eternal Love! Blessed be all those who, day after day, with undiminished generosity, accept your invitation, O

Mother, to do what your Jesus tells them (cf Jn 2:5) and give the Church and the world a serene testimony of lives inspired by the Gospel.

Above all, blessed be you, the Handmaid of the Lord, who in the fullest way obey the divine call!

Hail to you, who are wholly united to the redeeming consecration of your Son!

Mother of the Church! Enlighten the People of God along the paths of faith, of hope and love! Help us to live with the whole truth of the consecration of Christ for the entire human family of the modern world.

## AMI PRESS BOOK LIST

(Books marked with an * are hardcovers.)

All the books listed above and other titles are available from the Blue Army supply shop. Request ordering and price information by writing to:

**The Blue Army**
**Mountain View Road**
**Washington, N.J. 07882**

— NOTES —